# GOD

## IT'S NICE TO FINALLY MEET YOU

# GOD

## IT'S NICE TO FINALLY MEET YOU

How I met God in the midst of anxiety,
depression, self-doubt, and more.

## MONICA TOOKES

Tookes Time, LLC
*God, It's Nice to Finally Meet You*
Copyright © 2022 by Monica Tookes

Requests for information should be addressed to:
Tookes Time, LLC | info@tookestime.com | www.tookestime.com

Unless otherwise notes, all scripture quotations are taken from the Amplified Bible. Copyright © 2015 by The Lockman Foundation, La Habra, CA 90631. All rights reserved. Used by permission.

Scripture quotations marked NKJV are taken from the New King James Version Bible. Copyright © 1982 Thomas Nelson. All rights reserved. Used by permission.

Scripture quotations marked ESV are taken from the English Standard Version Bible. Copyright © 2001 by Crossway, a publishing ministry of Good News Publishers. All rights reserved. Used by permission.

Published by Tookes Time, LLC
Designed by
Edited by New Pointe Editing
Library of Congress Cataloging-in-Publication Data has been applied for:

ISBN: 979-8-9868744-0-1
E-book ISBN: 979-8-9868744-1-8

# DEDICATION

## TO MOM AND DAD

Thank you for being my greatest teachers and always encouraging me to pursue my dreams. I am blessed to have two loving parents that sacrificed so much to give me an opportunity to become the woman I am today. I love you both from the bottom of my heart, and I am grateful that God chose you two to be my parents.

## TO MY SIBLINGS

Being the baby of seven leaves some massive shoes to fill, but each of you has shown me that life is all about living your dreams. Thank you for being the best role models and always being there to support your little sis.

## TO MY VILLAGE

It truly does take a village to raise a child. Thank you for your part in shaping me into the woman that I am today. I pray God pours back into you everything you have poured into me (and more)!

## TO GOD

God, thank you for never giving up on me and constantly tugging at my heart every time I walked away from you. Meeting you was the best thing that ever happened because it allowed me to get to know you personally. I remember thinking that my life was over, but you said otherwise. The devil did everything he could to prevent me from discovering my purpose. He thought he won when I was depressed, full of self-doubt, and determined to quit on life. The enemy never stood a chance because you were always right by my side, even when I did not recognize you. Thank you for saving me through your son Jesus Christ and resurrecting me into the woman you always created me to be.

Thank you for leading me out of darkness so I could shine your light and bring others out of similar places I was once in. You called me to help women overcome the same challenges I battled and empower them to identify and ACTIVATE their God-given purpose. It's because of you that Women in Action was formed. I pray you get the glory out of everything I do and continue using me as your vessel. I will keep my eyes on you no matter how tough life gets. Turning back is not an option after finally meeting you!

## ENCOURAGING SCRIPTURES FROM MY VILLAGE

**Wanda Tookes (Mom)**
Isaiah 41:10

**Ronald Tookes (Dad)**
Exodus 20:12

**Toddrick (Brother)**
2 Corinthians 4:16-18

**Ronnie (Brother)**
Micah 4:5

**Jonathan (Brother)**
Philippians 4:13

**Sam (Brother)**
Exodus 20:12

**Rhonda (Sister)**
1 Corinthians 13:13

**Briana (Sister)**
Romans 8:28

**Uncle Cedric**
Psalm 23

**Tawanya Norwood**
Proverbs 17:17

**Alton Breeden**
2 Corinthians 5:17

**Sharon Breeden**
Isaiah 58:12

**Audrey Mason**
Psalm 23:4

**Ms. Margaret**
Proverbs 22:6

**Briah Thomas**
Philippians 4:6-7/Serenity

**Sebrena Thomas**
Philippians 4:13

**Timika Scott**
Philippians 4:13

**Ernestine Stone**
2 Timothy 2:15

**Samantha Laguerre**
Philippians 1:6

**Koreen Clarke**
Philippians 4:13

**Gabrielle Teate**
Proverbs 3:5-6

**Jamisse Gordon**
Isaiah 40:31

**Lady Alicia Johnson**
Jeremiah 29:11

**Rechelle Fleneury**
Isaiah 26:3

**Carolyn Edwards**
Ephesians 2:10

**Joan Rivera**
Isaiah 40:31

**Gisell Tejada**
Isaiah 40:31

**Tamieyah Johnson**
James 1:2-3

**Jasmine Carey**
Proverbs 4:2
**Jennifer Johnson**
Philippians 4:6-7
**Kristan Boyer**
Jeremiah 29:11

**Deborah Jackson**
Proverbs 3:5-6
**Schcola Chambers**
Isaiah 41:10
**Bianca Wilson**
2 Timothy 1:7

# ACKNOWLEDGING WOMEN IN ACTION

**Business Name**
Tookes Time, LLC
**Owner**
Monica Tookes
Author | Coach | Speaker
**Purpose**
God | Family | Education
I help women overcome self-doubt by empowering them to identify and
ACTIVATE their God-given purpose.
**Scan Me**

---

**Business Name**
Brick by Brick Experience
**Owner**
Min. Rechelle Fleneury
**Purpose**
I help women clarify their path to purpose in God and move from a
victim to victory mindset by unleashing the power of their voices found
through their unique life experiences.
**Scan Me**

# ACKNOWLEDGING WOMEN IN ACTION

**Business Name**
New Pointe Editing
**Owner**
Georgie Ann-Neil
**Purpose**
New Pointe Editing is committed to providing superior, personalized services that will enhance your written work for you, your business, and your brand.
**Scan Me**

---

**Business Name**
Charlene Money Coach
**Owner**
Charlene Tilbanie
**Purpose**
I help female Christian professionals and solopreneurs gain a Biblical perspective of kingdom wealth and use their faith + money to gain financial freedom WHILE honoring God.
**Scan Me**

# ACKNOWLEDGING WOMEN IN ACTION

**Ministry Name**
Women Who Will Ministries Inc.
**Founders**
Amber Adams & Arielle Brown
**Purpose**
At Women Who Will Ministries, our vision is to provide a global platform for a community of Women Who Will learn and apply the principles and promises of the Bible within their everyday lives empowering them to grow into the women God purposed them to become.
**Scan Me**

----------------------------------------------------------------

GRAD ON PURPOSE, LLC

**Business Name**
Grad on Purpose, LLC
**Owner**
Jessica Ross
**Purpose**
I serve purpose-driven recent grads and seasoned professionals who are ready to take their education and career to the next level, through career development resources and college application support services.
**Scan Me**

# ACKNOWLEDGING WOMEN IN ACTION

**Business Name**
The Daily Life Planner
**Founder**
Gabbriella Gabbidon
**Purpose**
The Daily Life Planner is a mindfully crafted planner designed to help you reach your target goals and dreams through organization, motivation, reflection, and prayer.
**Scan Me**

----------------------------------------------------------------------------

**Founder**
Keonna Shaw
**Purpose**
I equip Christian Women to Walk Confidently in Christ, Bloom in their Faith, and Build Intimacy with God.
**Scan Me**

# CONTENTS

❧

# NOTE FROM THE AUTHOR

Congratulations on being part of the 3% of people who read the books they purchase. Continue reading to see how I went from meeting God to embracing my new identity in Christ and ACTIVATING my God-given purpose. Part of my purpose is to empower you to walk in yours. As I use this book to share my life story, I will speak life into you. Just know that your journey with me does not have to end here. I encourage you to join my free Facebook group entitled Women in ACTION. Be part of a community where we pray, hold each other accountable, and study God's word together.

At the time of writing this book, I am offering a free clarity call for individuals serious about ACTIVATING their God-given purpose (price is subject to change). I encourage you to book a call with me today if you battle with any of the following: self-doubt, chronic worry, procrastination, inconsistency, or face any other mental barriers that may be hindering you from walking in your purpose. There is so much greatness in you; God is ready to ACTIVATE it through a personal relationship with Him. The question is, are you?

*Disclaimer: The free clarity call offer may no longer be in effect.*

*Introduction*

# MY STORY

M eeting God has been a life-altering experience that I would not trade for the world. I must admit, it took twenty-two years for me to recognize God's hand in my life. I spent most of my childhood learning about a God I did not know personally. I wanted to believe that He existed, but I did not understand how life could be so chaotic when there was supposedly a powerful God holding the world in His hands. Where was He when I wept in the middle of the night, when my aunt passed away, or when my family fell apart? These questions had me in a chokehold because I desperately sought answers that I could never find on my own.

Have you ever felt like life throws one curve ball after the other making it almost impossible for you to catch a break? Yeah, me too! I aimlessly attempted to dodge the trials of life by leaning onto my own understanding. The Bible warns us against this in Proverbs 3:5-6. Trying to avoid trials only subjected me to more trouble. I battled depression, anxiety, suicidal thoughts, self-doubt, and much more. I spent many years falling into shame and guilt, which only yanked me further from God's truth. God always desired an intimate love relationship with me, but I overlooked His invitation every time I focused on my problems versus His power.

I now understand that there is no condemnation in Christ Jesus. God wanted me to turn to Him, so He could heal, restore, and transform my life. This book is about an encounter with God and how that moment introduced me to my new identity in Christ. I am writing this book to encourage, inspire, and empower you to seek a relationship with God for yourself. My story may not be pretty, but it's full of purpose!

*Part 1*

---

# ACKNOWLEDGE

❧

## Chapter 1

# ENOUGH IS ENOUGH

Praying to a God that you were conditioned to serve from the time you entered this world does not seem ideal when forced. The intentions behind being sent to church religiously were pure and purposeful. My parents wanted to ensure that they exposed me to the same God that delivered and guided them into who they are and who they are becoming. For the longest, I could not identify with their experiences or reasoning for devoting their lives to an invisible god, especially when I witnessed some of the turmoil and effects of their trauma that refused to unleash them. I remember watching my mother unconsciously go into autopilot. The flight of life was bumpy, and the turbulence was high, but somehow, she walked away unscathed. I always yearned to reach that level of strength. However, I failed to realize that strength was merely a product of the struggles she had to face.

Growing up, I knew of God, but I did not know Him for myself nor understood His methods. My counsel came secondhand, and I was supposed to connect with others' perceptions of Him. My mom spent her life serving God, and I knew of Him because of her sincere and infectious prayers. So much power exuded from her lips every time she spoke to God. With age, I noticed that her pain is what made her prayers so powerful. My mother took her pain to God, but sometimes she neglected to leave it there. Instead, she often took the weight back and piled it on other underlying issues and sometimes on the people she loved. I witnessed this throughout my life and observed how her anger, resentment, and sadness pierced through her words.

On the other hand, I knew that my mother was loving, gentle, caring, compassionate, and a faithful servant of God. Devoting her time, talent, and treasure was normal, and she did not veer away from that. She went to church faithfully and found pleasure in serving others, but her life behind the scenes seemed to remain the same. My mother tried to make the best out of life, but I felt the odds were always stacked against her. I did not understand this contradiction because I witnessed the light radiating from my mom, and I walked with her through the darkness. This was when I began to doubt God and His existence.

After attending church countless Sundays, I started formulating expectations for God based on my interpretation of the lessons I learned in church. Many were founded on religious principles versus a personal love relationship with God. In my teens, I began to rebel against my parents and what I learned in the church because nothing made sense. Why would I serve God when my family went from being tightly knit to completely torn apart? I always blamed God for that until I finally met Him and learned about God's will versus our own.

I was blaming God for my family's faulty structure without considering the foundation on which it was built. That was the ultimate problem. How could I expect God to fix something He did not put together? My family would only be unified if we allowed God to return to the drawing board and put the pieces together as He originally intended. As easy as that sounds, that option was nonexistent for years because everyone in my family was focused on doing their own thing. We were the family of escapes, the founders of the original escape room. Except the room was our life, and the goal was to escape our problems with no will to return.

As I got older, I realized that my parents were my first example of being human. My dad was a true provider and would do anything to give us the world. I did not understand the pressure behind being a Black male as a child. My father had a "make it happen" mentality, and his motives were pure. However, the pressure that came with that motto was sometimes too heavy to bear. Growing up, I judged my father greatly, not realizing that he was flesh like me. My dad was looking for the love and affection my mother never received, so he found other ways to meet his needs. He found satisfaction in his job and dedicated most of his time to the community. I would get frustrated because I felt like he spent more time with strangers than with his family. Leaving me to feel abandoned when he was operating out of purpose. I did not focus on how he built relationships in the community and brought peace and joy to everyone he met. I did not see my dad for who he was. I would get upset that he was not present during my teenage years, but I did not consider who was present during his. Sometimes parents do what they think is best for their children, often modeling their own childhood.

My parents were learning on the fly, and I must admit, they did an amazing job with what they had. God was working in and through them their entire lives. I thought I was going through issues that they never had to face. What a misconception! We faced the same problems. I was just the first to talk about it openly. God used me to start the dialogue so we could heal together. When I met God through His son Jesus, I realized that God cares about my family. He intentionally created and placed us right where we are. I understand this now, but that was not always the case.

My mom is the prayer warrior of the family. I heard her pray faithfully at the break of dawn daily. She repeatedly said "Heavenly Father " as she prayed, and it did not take long for me to conclude that she was referring to God. My mother's prayers permeated the power of God every time she parted her lips. The only thing I did not understand was how she could know God and still be full of so much pain. I expected God to remove all of that and prevent her from experiencing anything else that could weigh her down. I felt like she endured enough as a child and did not need any more pressure as an adult. I did not understand that the pressure and pain were what gave her purpose.

I knew my expectations for God were unrealistic when I started discovering some of the same wounds from my mom's life within myself. I became angry, bitter, sad, and easily irritated, which was odd because I always had a bright spirit. The shift began when my parents started feuding and when we made a sudden move to a new city. There was no time to process the changes and why they happened so abruptly. My parents tried their best to shield my siblings and me from the logistics of their issues. We may not have known the details, but that did not protect us against the root cause or effect of their pain.

Children have a level of innocence that is gradually discarded as they begin to learn the ways of the world through what they are exposed to. I know my parents wanted to protect my siblings and I from their problems, but that only fueled the generational curses that yearned to choke our innocence while projecting the same patterns of my family's past. I did not see what was going on behind closed doors, but I detected and battled against the same spirits throughout my life. I learned about God in the church but did not hear about the demons I would have to face or how I could fight against them. My lack of understanding led to a quandary that caused me to make assumptions and fill in the blanks to questions without human answers. Hence my reasoning for projecting blame onto God, the church, and eventually my family.

As a teenager, I battled rejection, depression, anxiety, suicidal thoughts, pornography, drugs, and much more. Being seen as the "perfect" child forces you to try to fit the mold. So, I hid all my pain, trying to live up to everyone else's false expectations. I felt the need to be strong like my mother, which meant I could not afford to show any signs of weakness. Everyone celebrated my false image of perfection, and my pride basked in it even though I was tearing apart on the inside. As I got older, I started to question the purpose of the church. I could not understand why no one saw me suffering in silence. Eventually, I concluded that the church could not help me, and I needed to figure things out alone. This was when I was introduced to alcohol, porn, and dating. Almost as if the enemy served it on a silver platter. It all looked good initially until those vices no longer satisfied my immediate craving. I went from one extreme to the next, trying to be fulfilled, and was only left feeling hopeless, drained, and unworthy, which is right where the enemy wanted me.

I could not relate to the level of perfection presented in the church. That was the lens that I chose to look through, which led to my interpretation. In hindsight, no one claimed to be perfect. Yet, I expected them to be because they claimed to know this powerful God. A part of me wanted to see an alternative to what I was experiencing. Blinders of judgment, comparison, and envy blocked my view of God and how He was moving. Not just in the lives of others but in my life.

It turns out that many people in my life pretended to be perfect to avoid the judgment of others. When I looked at believers in the church, I could see past the mask they effortlessly applied every Sunday because I had my own mask. My smile in the sanctuary did not match the silent cries behind the bathroom stalls. After years of going through the motions, I could no longer put on a facade. My heart was shattered, and I did not know how it had happened.

After a while, I could no longer judge anyone in the church for not being authentic because I became a reflection of them. Lack of wisdom and understanding stunts our spiritual, mental, and emotional growth. I witnessed a group of people with stunted growth in the church, including myself. We tried to hide the things we did not understand and held onto what made us feel comfortable. Comfort led to complacency, and we learned to operate this way versus allowing God to heal our wounds, help us understand the effects of our trauma, and instruct us on how to move forward. My spiritual immaturity made it difficult to hear the voice of God, and I often spoke over it with human wisdom or ignored it due to distractions. I realized all this, and instead of taking my issues to God, I continued to doubt Him because my family followed Him for years, and I felt like it never got us anywhere. I blamed God for my pain because he watched me suffer without coming to my rescue.

After trying things my way and repeating what I witnessed growing up, I realized that was not working for me. I was on a path of self-destruction, and I did not know where to find the abort button. I remember thinking enough is enough! Instead of going to the church and asking someone to pray for me, I went to God personally. I opened my mouth and spewed the power of my mother's prayers. The taste was eerie, but I continued because it felt good releasing my pain to the one I thought caused it. My prayer was not cute or formal. It was the most disrespectful encounter I have ever had. Tears began to inundate my face, and my truth enlightened me, and the weight of imperfection began to lift off my shoulders. For the first time, I wanted to run, and at that moment, I understood the people that ran like track stars in church. While laying my heart out to God, I heard myself say everything that caused me to doubt His existence. I then realized that each thought had one commonality, my lack of understanding.

I noticed that I was blaming God for my incapacity to make sense of His will and my inability to refrain from sin, which was influenced by the adversaries' deceit. This revelation let me know that I needed to give God another try and let go of this mindset I had developed over the years. The problem was not God. I became the issue when I allowed sin, lack of understanding, and the enemy's tactics to overcome me.

# Dear Reader

---

You have the choice to leave behind anything that has been bringing you down. You may have experienced abandonment, rejection, abuse, manipulation, heartbreak, disappointment, grief, etc. Please know that God can repurpose your pain. But He can only do that when you get fed up with the enemy's lies and say, enough is enough!

So many people opened their lives up to others and were left disappointed when their expectations were not met. We are all human, which makes us imperfect beings. However, God is perfect, and so is His son Jesus. This book is meant to guide you to your encounter with Christ. I pray that some part of my story will encourage, inspire, or motivate you to draw closer to God.

Nothing you experience in life is too hard for God. He wants to lead, guide, teach, counsel, and provide for you. Know that God will not force you to follow or believe in Him. Though He stands at the door and knocks, you must let Him in. You may have tried everything else with no positive results in sight. I implore you to try Jesus. God is knocking today. Will you let Him into your life?

## Chapter 2

# GETTING TO THE ROOT

Every tree goes through seasons, and it is interesting how the fruit reflects the condition of the roots. For years, I tried to hide my rotten roots while maintaining a healthy life, at least one that appeared that way. But what does healthy even mean? Our interpretation only comes from what we were taught. Often, we were just a product of someone else's dying roots. I do not know much about plants, but there are enough green thumbs on Instagram for me to see that you can take part of the roots from one plant to start another. Google says that this is a process called propagating. Being "propagated" is cool until you are bred from a parent plant that was barely surviving in the first place.

You could say that I grew up in a "dysfunctional" household. As an emotional teenage girl, I would be ready to shout how messed up my life was from the rooftops. But, in hindsight, it was not too bad at all. I had two parents that loved me dearly and jumped at any opportunity to show it. My perspective as an adult has shifted, but I had to experience a lot to see life through a clearer lens. Our family roots may have been damaged, but they were not dead. I gained this perspective when I started getting to the root of my issues, which mirrored my family's roots.

I call us dysfunctional because we went through a spiritual drought that affected everything else in our lives. My momma covered the family for years, attempting to carry the living water independently. She was far from perfect, reminding me of Hannah from 1 Samuel in the Bible. I know hell was shaken the moment my mom learned how to pray. My great grand momma, Tiny Bell, would send her, my aunt (TT), and my uncle Cedric down to the church on the corner when they were growing up. My momma did not depart from what she learned about God. She had many imperfect trainers, but she learned from the best to do it! Jesus! Walking to that church on the corner every week imparted something that is still impactful to this day. Momma made sure we went to church every Sunday and whenever the church doors were open. I was also trained up as a child but departed with no will to return. That was until I met Jesus for myself.

Our family roots were damaged because we had some diseases that led to a destiny of death. Dysfunction is the root of congregated pain, a disease that tried to girdle my family. A disease sent by the enemy on assignment to kill, steal, and destroy everything God created us to be. Despite his efforts, we were kept by the grace of God channeled through my mother's prayers. I did not understand this as a child, but now I can see.

I recall Sunday dinners after church, daddy-daughter dates, and my momma blowing my neck as she pressed my naps using the hot comb from the stove. My childhood memories are endless, and I would not trade them for the world. My parents did everything to provide the best life for my siblings and me. They trained us up to serve the Lord and met our every need. My oblivion prevented me from seeing what was happening behind the scenes.

What happens when you are no longer protected by superficial armor and what you were conditioned to believe wears off? Your perspective begins to shift as ignorance is replaced with awareness. For example, as I got older, I realized that my family had a lot of issues, and I thought I could fix them by being the perfect child. Almost as if my falsified perfection would heal their pain.

My savior mentality started at a young age. Growing up, I learned so much about Jesus that I tried to do what he already died for. Seeing my family struggle made me internalize our problems, and I always felt responsible for fixing them. Hide daddy's keys, so he does not leave again, get up early and see momma because she is sad, do my chores for my brothers because they were busy, save to buy nicotine gum for TT so she would stop smoking, and the list goes on. I always believed that I needed to support everyone else and be mindful of how my problems could potentially affect others. Therefore, I pretended like everything was okay even though I started falling apart on the inside. I went to church every Sunday, sang in the choir, ushered, and danced. I sang about God's grace and mercy but could not recognize it. I had a village that helped raise me and led me on the right path, but they could not save me. Only God could, and I veered away from Him as I got older.

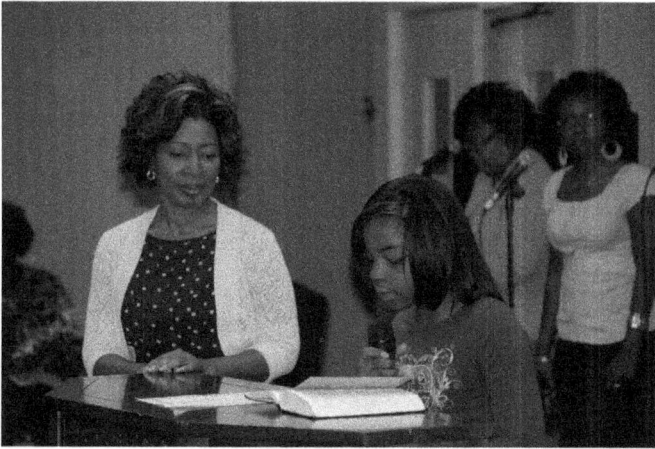

Like the rest of my family, I learned to suppress my pain and go on as if it never existed. I never discussed my feelings, how my aunt's death affected me, or how upset I was when my dad moved away. I downplayed my emotions because I felt I was supposed to bear it all alone. I went to church every week, and there were times when I just sat in the pew and cried. Especially during praise and worship. I kept hearing about a God that moves mountains, breaks chains, will never let me down, is a healer, faithful, and is all-knowing—that led me to believe He saw me and understood my pain. Have you ever felt like God was allowing you to suffer? I surely did, and I believed He found satisfaction in my misery. However, that was far from the truth. God wanted to provide consolation, but I rejected it because I thought God rejected me every time I prayed, and my suffering did not cease.

The devil planted the seed of rejection and watered it when my father left home, my relationships ended, and I failed to fit into any crowd—causing insecurity, fear, and a false identity to sprout, eventually turning into a tree of death. To the world, my fruit appeared fresh, but I was truly rotting on the inside. My innocence escaped me as I tried to cling to any form of acceptance I could find. The enemy convinced me that I was rejected when I was being redirected toward God. Instead, I turned away because I expected God to fix my problems while I continued to live as I pleased, and that is not how He operates. I had this expectation for years until I realized that my issues only intensified over time. That is when I started taking matters into my own hands and finding ways to escape my problems.

How many people reposition themself out of the passenger seat and take the wheel when they feel like they can drive the car better than someone else? They took too many detours, drove too slowly, went over too many speed bumps, etc. Whatever the case, this is exactly what I did with God. I did not move Him to the passenger seat, though. Instead, I kicked Him out of my car (my life) and sped off, thinking I would get to my destination faster. I never detected that my car would be totaled along the way due to my haste and collision with the adversary and his divisive tactics.

As I sped off into my life journey, the church was the last place I wanted to go, but I knew I had no other options. I grew up hearing my momma say, "As long as you are in this house, you will serve the Lord!" So, I kept wearing my mask of flawlessness until I had a valid excuse not to go. I was not upset with the people in the church, I was upset with God, and I could not wait to leave Him and everything else He stood for. As for Jesus, I wanted to be close with Him and share how I felt, but I figured He wanted nothing to do with me because I rejected His father. First, I did not understand the Godhead because I thought of God and Jesus as two separate people, and the Holy Spirit was nowhere on my radar. I looked up to Jesus without realizing that God worked in and through Him throughout His life. Every Easter, I would get upset with God because I could not see the bigger picture. I thought God abandoned Jesus on the cross when in reality, God is the one who took every lash, thorn, and nail. Not to mention raising Jesus from the dead and being intentional enough to leave us with His spirit! My misunderstanding led to resentment, and I started looking to the world for comfort.

At nine, I was introduced to my sexuality, and my lack of understanding heightened my curiosity. I had no desire to have sex, but I held it in the back of my mind and thought of it as leverage to get what I wanted if necessary. In middle school, my best friend introduced me to pornography, and my innocence was sucked away with every second I indulged. An invisible enemy named lust came from the confines of my computer screen. Sin crept from my eyes to my hands which resorted to self-gratification, welcoming the spirit of perversion. The temporary satisfaction was not worth the demons I would have to fight eventually.

Growing up in church, I learned that my body was pure and I should save sex until marriage. I wanted to honor that until I stopped believing that God was honoring His word, and at that point, all bets were off. So, my new boyfriend and I had sex, and after a few minutes, my purity was gone. I remember laying there, inwardly waving my cherry goodbye as he started to wipe the area where my sexual immorality began. I almost felt like it was my way of getting back at God and doing something that made me feel free. I was on a high that I thought would last for eternity. When my mom found out, I was brought back to life, and the guy completely ghosted me. I did not understand how someone could be so cold and leave without an explanation. His departure only reminded me of my father's absence, which added to my frustration. I did not talk to my mom about how I felt because I started to blame her for pushing him away, just like she did my father. I am convinced that the teenage brain is a curse because my logic was far from the truth. This was the start of me blaming others and not taking responsibility for my actions. I repeated this cycle, which got me nowhere except depressed and full of regret.

After that incident, I continued looking for men to love me, and I felt I needed to try a different approach. The next guy I met had no chance of having sex with me. I met him at an away game for a track meet. He was charismatic, and I got butterflies every time we talked. Our "talking" phase lasted for about three weeks, and one night we started kissing, which led to the very thing I was trying to avoid. I remember tears streaming toward my ears as I lay there because I knew he would leave me just like the last guy. I was giving my body away again for nothing. After that encounter, I became numb to sex and continued allowing him to use my body as his object because it became leverage. He asked me to be his girlfriend after we had sex, and I agreed. What more did I have to lose? Everything! I was so desperate that I did not even recognize the detriment of my decisions and how they affected me.

I was giving my body and heart to everyone except for God. That shows how upset I was with Him, exactly where the enemy wanted me. He was successful at his job and left me where I was mentally doing his job for him. I started talking down on myself. I had no self-esteem and no longer cared about anyone or anything. Imagine God standing with open arms and me turning in the opposite direction, looking for something greater than Him. It took me a few years of trying and failing to recognize that there is no one and nothing greater than God. I wanted to be loved, but I searched for it in the wrong places, like many of us, before accepting God's everlasting love.

After a few months of trying to finish up my junior year in high school, taking dual enrollment classes, and maintaining a long-distance relationship, I felt overwhelmed, and anxiety began to creep in. I was sixteen and battling all of this by myself, which pushed me further into the arms of a boy that claimed to love me but did not even know what love was. Truthfully, neither of us had a clue, and pretending was all we knew. We kept fornicating, and my parents knew nothing about him. My dad moved out of the house, and my mom was busy working. Some may say I was looking for attention, and they would not be wrong. This ordeal lasted until I started having severe abdominal pains. My boyfriend had given me an STD, and at that point, I was done! Here is the kicker, after uncivilly telling him he didn't even care! Anger, rage, and distress devoured me to the point where I was unrecognizable. Guess who I blamed? Of course, the boy, but I also blamed God. Looking back, I have no clue how I could blame God when I chose to be with the boy in the first place. I was so upset with God back then that I never acknowledged or thanked Him for preventing me from contracting something that was not treatable... that was the epitome of grace! I may not have known God, but He knew enough about me to cover me despite my disobedience.

Eventually, I got old enough to apply for a job, and it became my first excuse to leave the church when I was hired. While still in high school, I deviated from sports and started working long hours to help get my mind away from what I was going through. When I graduated from high school, I thought I would be able to escape everything by going off to college. After applying to four schools, I received three acceptance letters and a rejection letter from the school I felt led to. I did not understand why because I had over a 4.0 GPA. I was so focused on guys that I neglected to put much effort into my ACT. My desperation to move and have a chance at a fresh start made me consider settling for one of the other schools that accepted me. However, nothing seemed to work out, and everything felt forced. So, I went to the community college near my house and kept working at Red Lobster. Defeat consumed me, and I was embarrassed because I believed people would view me differently. My pride led me to apply for three other jobs to redeem myself, and I got each of them. Working became my escape. I was so busy that I did not have time to focus on my problems.

Working hard was my priority, and I kept this up for a few months while single. Honestly, I did not have time for a relationship, and I was still dwelling on the effects of my last two. Then I met this cook at my job, and he was interested in getting to know me. For the sake of confidentiality, let's call him Tim. I was reluctant and had no intentions of starting anything new. However, Tim was persistent, so I finally allowed him to take me on a date. I learned he was gentle, compassionate, a great listener, and genuinely cared about my interests. I was skeptical and kept wondering what the catch was. You may have guessed it. He had a child. His son was ten years old, only seven years younger than me. Tim was twenty-six, and I was fond of his age because I was tired of dealing with boys. Truthfully, I was just being grown and subconsciously subjecting myself to another broken soul in my aimless pursuit of love. One date led to two, and that led to another relationship. I convinced myself that his son did not affect me because he did not live nearby.

I was sure that I finally found love. Tim was gentle and patient; he did not raise his voice, pressure me for sex, or make me feel uncomfortable. He put my needs and desires before his own, which I was not accustomed to. Now I understand that he was a mirrored image of me. We were both entering a relationship to escape our trauma and failing to realize how that would only lead us to project our issues onto one another. One of those was pretending to be something that we weren't. I was pleased with his production because it aligned with my superficial expectation of love. I got what I wanted and felt the need to show gratitude. So again, sex became a natural element, creating a soul tie that my flesh found pleasure in but would soon come to despise. He fell deeply in love with me, and I verbally reciprocated that. However, my heart was truly not in it, especially when I discovered he had a second child on the way that was conceived before we started dating. I should have left with that news, but I decided to stay and pretend to be a supportive girlfriend.

I was going through the motions and pretending to be in love while dying inwardly. I remember meeting the mother of his child, staring at her belly, and imagining the life she was about to bring into the world. My imagination morphed into reality on the day when I was scheduled to get on birth control. Tim agreed to go with me for support but had to back out because the mother of his child was in labor. So, I was in the doctor's office by myself, mentally rehearsing how I was preventing myself from having a child while he was watching his second enter this world. That did not sit right with me, but I did it anyway because I knew I was not ready to have children. I am glad I listened to that voice because I would have been baby momma number three, miserable, and stuck in a relationship with someone I did not love. I remember going to the hospital after the doctor injected a rod into my arm, which left me with a scar that could not heal. I asked the receptionist for the labor and delivery unit, and she asked me for the mother's name. That is when everything became real. I did not know the mother's name, had no desire to know, and had no business at that hospital. My boyfriend came down and got me after I called him, and my heart sank as I entered the room. A beautiful baby girl was swaddled in the arms of my boyfriend's mother, and where everyone was full of joy, I was full of sorrow. I held her for a minute, and my eyes began to swell up with tears, so I handed her off and left abruptly. I sat in my car and cried because I thought I had found the perfect person for me, but everything changed when I saw him bring his baby girl into the world.

I ended up staying in that relationship while being depressed and miserable. He was in my comfort zone, but nothing about that relationship brought comfort to me, except for the sin I indulged in to help me cope. I started smoking, constantly having sex, and drinking my life away. I no longer went to church, so I did not have to pretend to be okay. My mom noticed a change in my behavior and continued to pray, but it was almost as if the devil taunted her as my depression grew. I would come home drunk and high almost every night after working over 16 hours and going to my boyfriend's house to do my dirt. I was falling into the devil's rabbit hole of deception to the point where I felt like I was drowning. Over time, the enemy convinced me that I had no reason to live and that no one would miss me if I died. That led me to believe that death was my best option, so suicidal thoughts continuously swarmed my mind. Thank God for my mother's prayers. I know those were the only things that kept me. Finally, one night, my mom found me in the kitchen with a butcher knife, and I was about to slit my wrists. She just began to cry out to God and rebuke the devil. Suddenly, I snapped out of his deception, stared at the knife in my hand, and started to wail. I knew I had to make drastic changes because I was on the verge of ending my life.

Do you see how the enemy tries to slither into your life by presenting something that looks good externally? He did it to Eve in the garden of Eden, which initiated the curse of sin that Jesus had to come and die for. The devil convinced me that my father had abandoned me, and I needed to find acceptance and love elsewhere. The devil used shame to convince me that God wanted nothing to do with me. Even though that was far from the truth, Jesus died so that we may live more abundantly! Looking back, I recognize that I was repeating a cycle. I was searching for the unconditional love that only God could give me.

## Chapter 3

# WHAT NOW?

I knew what I witnessed in the church was the effect of surviving in this brutal world another day. I also saw the veil of flawlessness that people effortlessly applied to avoid the judgment of others. As much as I despised this, I failed to see how I followed them. After watching my family struggle in private while simultaneously presenting perfection to the world, I learned how to go beyond the surface level. What meets the eye is misleading, and my understanding of this at a young age led to a quest to identify everyone else's pain points—not recognizing how that would inevitably create some of my own through a funnel of generational curses that I was oblivious to.

My first encounter with God did not come as expected. I always thought I had to be within the church's walls to experience the Lord. God was not present if people were not shouting or running like track stars. I was misled because I met Him for the first time in the same room where my depression and anxiety dwelled. At church, I learned to wear a mask and pretend everything was smooth sailing because I had God on my side. However, that was far from the truth.

I went to church all of my life, and at the age of twenty-two, I still could not connect with whatever God they spoke of in church. I had countless questions that I desperately needed answers to. Half of them were considered taboo, and I knew not to utter my inquiries around Christians because I would be reminded of my sins and have the Bible thrown back in my face. That was upsetting, but the people who gave me those responses did so because those were the same answers they received. We were taught not to question certain things, leaving many Christians pretending to believe their curiosity diminished when they chose to follow God.

At the age of fourteen, I stopped trying to live up to the expectations of this invisible god. I felt like I was sacrificing everything while getting nothing and being told to be thankful for the same life I once attempted to take. I was not supposed to have sex, go to church faithfully, give my talents to the church, read my Bible, pray, and even fast. I saw a lot of deposits with no return on my investment. The thought of this daunting commitment contributed to my reluctance to follow God wholeheartedly. This made me question who this God was. I watched my parents faithfully attend church and cut a check every time we entered the doors. Yet, I did not understand why. Our home was a fiasco, but we pretended everything was perfect in public. We learned to cast our cares upon the Lord in the church because he cares for us. That was laughable. He did not seem to care when my parents were feuding or when He ignored all of my prayers. I asked for a unified family, and I got the exact opposite.

Our perspective plays a major role in how we view God. I was so caught up in what was going wrong in my life that I failed to see what was going right. My parents went to church faithfully because they wanted to thank God for all the times He saved and covered them. When my mom was nearly homeless, God made a way for her. They also praised God for covering me. The devil was trying to take me out since conception like he did my older brother, that never made it here on this side of the earth due to an ectopic pregnancy. I am a walking miracle, but I was so blindsided by deception that I could not see God's blessings. Despite how rebellious I became, I still felt convicted because I was constantly reminded of what I learned in church, and I was not comfortable being outside God's will. Going against God felt good for a moment, but I was torn internally because I knew that I was contributing to my own demise through my disobedience and blatant disregard for God.

Early in life, I was the child that analyzed everything with hopes of making sense of it all. A task that I was passionate about doing but never successful at. Why did my mom serve an invisible god supposedly in charge of everything? That meant that He took her mother at the age of three. Why would He do that if He knew the repercussions I would witness firsthand through the cloud of depression that rained down on me through her trauma? I never received a clear answer, but I kept hearing that God was in control. I could not stop thinking that He was also in control of the division within my family.

One may ask, how can three words encompass so much anger and frustration? I remember screaming, "who are you!" and "where are you!" to this God I unwillingly devoted my life to. Growing up in the church was both a blessing and a curse. That applies to anything in life, and it depends on your perspective. The church was a blessing because the messages given penetrated your soul to the point where the feeling could still be accessed years later. It also provided a support system that was often taken for granted when I focused on the flaws of others versus identifying and dealing with my own. On the other hand, it was a curse when hypocrisy lingered like the devil lurking in the night.

The words that came from the church did not necessarily match up to the actions of the same people giving the word. I could not see God in the church because I was too focused on the actions of others that were not of God. I never realized that those same people I judged were flesh like me. None of us are perfect, but I was annoyed at how everyone pretended to be. I was accustomed to hearing "blessed and highly favored" in response to a casual check-in question. I wasn't bothered by the phrase but the fake mask that protruded from them when the words left their lips. I rarely heard anyone say that I am not doing too well, but God will get me through. Those were the words that I desperately needed to hear because I felt far from "blessed and highly favored." While asking God the questions, ``Where are you and who are you?" I did not realize that I had initiated the search necessary to find God. It turns out that God was never lost. I was. My spiritual journey began when I hit rock bottom, and God was the only option I had left.

# Dear Reader

❧

Know that God is watching over you; whatever you are going through is not too hard for Him. You may not know what is next for your life which is okay. God just wants you to come home to Him. This world is brutal, and it only offers death. Whatever satisfaction the world has to offer will never be sustained. However, when you learn about God and enter into a relationship with Him, you will soon realize that He has much more to offer. As a child of God, you can access healing, deliverance, everlasting life, joy, peace, love, and everything else you need. There is no scarcity in the Kingdom of God, so you shall not lack.

God does not have to be your last option for you to choose Him. God has already called and chosen you. All you must do is answer the call. Many of us fail to pick up because we have God blocked or on do not disturb. That does not stop Him from trying to get through. God will send you signs, opportunities, storms, people, and anything else to get your attention. The devil will do the same, trying to set up distractions. If you want to know what's next, focus on Jesus. He died, so you may one day see God. Not just in heaven, but see God on the inside of you.

*Chapter 4*

# THE ENCOUNTER

In the past, I never thought that I could encounter God. I always felt like He was out of reach, so I would only consult Him when I was desperate for something. Treating God like a quick fix only satisfied my fleshly urge for so long. I played myself because I unintentionally learned that God is far from transactional. When I realized this, I put God down like the dozen grocery bags we muster to carry in on one trip. I wanted things to be quick and easy, and if God did not move fast enough, Monica was there to save the day. At least, that is what I presumed to be true until my life started falling apart.

I felt like I was better off before accepting Christ as my Savior. This was contradictory because I thought life with God was supposed to be better. It turns out that I accepted Jesus Christ as my personal Savior, but it took a while to make Him Lord over my life. How could I give my life to someone I didn't even know? Salvation was a term I could not identify with because I thought it equated to freedom from suffering and pain. I failed to realize that there was a process I would go through, and I would still face the very thing

I wanted to be free from. Notice I did not mention wanting to be free from sin. Yet that is exactly what Jesus died for. When I decided to be a follower of Christ, I was unprepared for the spiritual battle I would have to face. There is no war between good and evil when you are a slave to sin, but everything changes when you confess your sins and turn toward Jesus. I was not ready for the conviction that came with salvation. So, I claimed to be saved while living with a grave mindset. Somehow, I still expected my life to change for the better because I gave my life to the Lord. I WAS INFURIATED when I dealt with the same issues after accepting the altar call.

Betrayal was all I felt, and I was distraught with God again. Repeatedly asking God the question, "WHERE ARE YOU?" I started viewing God the same way I looked at the people in the church. His actions were not matching up to the promises in His word. So, I left the church and did my own thing. I sought relationships for the love and security I felt I was not receiving from my father or God. My dad moved out of the house when I was a teenager, and I felt like everything in my life shifted. I never doubted his love for me, but I needed more than he had to offer. I came from a family of escapes where we found things to help us get our minds off of whatever was bothering us versus getting to the root. Leaving family to work and provide was my father's way of escaping internal issues he did not know how to express. His absence left me with a hole in my heart carved by abandonment which led to my own series of escapes.

It did not take long for me to develop a resentment for God that would last for years. Frustration prompted me to overwork myself and turn to coping mechanisms that only numbed my pain. I would go to work at six-thirty and leave at six in the evening. Then come home and have a vodka sprite with a splash of grenadine, or stuff the fattest cone with my favorite herb and puff my life away. That was my way of adapting and dealing with my pain. I felt alone, and the only company I welcomed was the slew of thoughts roaming through my head. The combination of avoidance and bitterness hurled me into a deep depression, almost suffocating. I could not foresee it then, but a mental breakdown was bound to happen, and when it did, I was not ready to deal with the repercussions. I started shutting myself off from close friends and family, began dwelling on my problems, and escaping them was no longer an option. Therefore, I wallowed in them, and depression and anxiety engulfed me like the flame that burns wood to its core. This lasted for almost two years, and no one would have known. Everyone thought I had it together, and I almost killed myself trying to fit that mold.

One thing the church taught me was how to put on a mask that looked as natural as a beat frontal. I became a master at hiding my emotions and pain. I learned to bottle everything up and bury it with my other underlying issues. This inevitably leads to anxiety which looks like a mound of emotions thrashing against you as you aimlessly try to shield yourself while gasping for air. That was the effect of avoiding trauma, hurt, pain, fears, insecurities, etc. Suppression only leads to depression because the wounds never heal. They just get covered up, causing them to infect other areas of our hearts. Depression was the effect of hiding and neglecting the root issues of abandonment, rejection, fear, and unforgiveness. As a young girl, I internalized my father leaving, being misused in relationships, and pretending as if nothing bothered me. In hindsight, I was intensifying the pain other people subjected me to.

Who knew that your childhood experiences were the foundation of your identity and gauge of self-worth? I surely did not. I could not recognize that some of those experiences stemmed from generational curses meant to end with me. How could that happen if that is what molded me into who I became? When I realized this, I started to understand that the depression and anxiety that hovered over me directly resulted from generational trauma that was never dealt with. I also started self-reflection, revealing that I chose to sin every time I stepped outside God's will. I thought doing things my way was better, but it plunged me into a rabbit hole that felt impossible to escape.

Unforgiveness opened the door of my heart to the enemy and allowed him to take precedence over my emotions, thoughts, and decisions. Many people are oblivious to how the enemy comes in with his deception, schemes, and lies. I always imagined the devil as a gruesome individual I would despise over time. In reality, the opposite was true. Satan was disguised in my relationships, my desires, and what I found pleasure in.

Ever wonder why sin feels so easy? The enemy has strategically altered your way of thinking because he could enter your heart through wounds that were never tended to. The enemy used the individual who lied to you or abused you as a way to get you to harden your heart and walk in unforgiveness. He targets the heart because he knows that is how he can get and keep us distant from God. That is the ultimate way the enemy comes to steal, kill, and destroy. Our hearts are connected to our minds which control our reasoning and decision-making. When we surrender our hearts to God, sin is no longer tempting because we learn how to resist the devil with God's guidance. Like many others, I did not understand this concept at the beginning of my spiritual journey. For years, I misplaced my anger when I started to blame God for my frustration versus recognizing how I allowed the enemy to manipulate me.

Being upset with God was pointless, and after a while, I concluded that He was not to be blamed for my issues. No one told me to leave the church, seek relationships with men out of desperation, close myself off from the people who loved me, or sulk about my issues. Those were all the choices that forced me to deal with depression and anxiety. I asked where God was, but I was never genuinely looking for Him. My human nature caused me to believe that God was supposed to show up in my life without me having to do the work. When I prayed, I expected an immediate answer or solution. I treated God as if he were some sort of genie that granted wishes upon request. Discovering this made me realize that I needed to take responsibility for my actions and give God another chance.

Initially, I felt like a hypocrite, and my guilt and shame made it difficult to turn to God. I felt He would reject or disown me because of my misdirected anger toward him. Then I remembered a scripture we learned in church, "For You, O Lord, are good, and ready to forgive [our sins, sending them away, completely letting them go forever and ever]; and abundant in lovingkindness and overflowing in mercy to all those who call upon You," stated in Psalm 86:5 (AMP). I also thought about the times I heard my mother cry out to God in prayer. Her prayers were not formal. She just laid her heart out to God as you would to someone you loved. So, despite my feelings about Him, I decided to give God another try.

This prayer was different from any of the others I expressed. Like Hannah, I cried out to God and verbally acknowledged everything weighing me down. Hannah's pain is what positioned her heart toward God. Her weeping turned into worship, which granted her heart's every desire. I wanted to know why God left me stranded by myself, why He would not come to rescue me, and ultimately why He was not appearing to be a God of His word. Then, I randomly got a notification on Facebook. It was a video of Le'Andria Johnson singing, Deliver Me. Tears immediately inundated my face. I curled up on the floor and repeatedly listened to this song. The song made me realize that despite my frustration with God, He was the only source that could deliver me from what I was experiencing. It was evident that my attempts were fruitless and in vain.

The song, Deliver Me helped me realize that I was hurting myself whenever I tried to take matters into my own hands. At this point, I concluded that I was the reason why my life was turned upside down. No one told me to stay at work for ten-plus hours, aimlessly enter relationships, or resort to vices for comfort. Instead, I was blaming God for the mess I made, and that is when I opened my eyes to the fact that God never stood a chance because I blamed him for my wrongdoing. Le'Andria's passion permeated my bedroom that night, and I kept hearing, "this is my exodus!" That line reminded me of the book of Exodus that we studied in church. I remember reading about the Israelites and how they were delivered out of Egypt. As a child, I did not understand, but at that moment, I knew I was like the Israelites. Instead of being released from Pharaoh, God was removing me from myself.

Before God could show up in my life, I had to acknowledge that I was not allowing God to intervene every time I abandoned His will for my own. So, I decided to surrender and release every pain point to God. As I listened to the song in my bedroom, I felt a presence in the room. There was peace in my release - the weight of guilt and shame began to lift from my shoulders. That night, I finally met Jesus, and His presence introduced me to God. I was consumed with the love of God, but I could not identify with the feeling. This ineffable moment was far greater than anything I had ever experienced. So, I laid there in the middle of my bedroom floor and cried myself to sleep.

# Dear Reader

———

*Ə*

**D**uring this season of my life, God revealed to me that I was trapped in a grave mindset. I was breathing, but my soul coded more times than I could count. No matter how hard I tried to get out of my spiritual tomb, I failed every time. At this point in my life, I was about to be introduced to someone I had heard about in church. Jesus. He was the only one that could save me and carry me out of bondage.

For anyone reading this book, please know that Jesus loves you no matter what your past may look like. Instead of allowing shame to turn you away from Him, allow your imperfection to turn you towards His grace, love, mercy, and peace. I only failed because I tried to get away from my reality without knowing an alternative. God is your alternative, and He has an entire Kingdom that He wants to give you access to through His son Jesus Christ. Learn from my mistakes and repent for your wrongdoings and ask that God create in you a clean heart where you can believe that His son Jesus died on the cross for your sins and allow Him to deliver you from anything that has been hindering you from who God has called you to be. The enemy only attacks us to prevent us from discovering our identity through Christ Jesus. Make the decision today to turn away from his deceit and accept the unmerited grace of Jesus Christ. Your sins were left on the cross where His blood was shed for you. As you continue reading, know that God has not given up on you, so please do not give up on yourself.

If you **believe** that Jesus Christ died on the cross for your sins and would like to invite Him into your heart to be your personal Lord and Savior, say this prayer. "Lord Jesus, I confess my sins and ask for your forgiveness. Please come into my heart as my Lord and Savior. Take complete control of my life and help me walk in Your footsteps daily by the power of the Holy Spirit. Thank you, Lord, for saving me and answering my prayer."

Please understand that this prayer activates a process and leads to transformation. Your salvation does not end with this prayer. It starts with a lifestyle change and committing your life to the Lord. God does not desire perfection; he wants your heart. The journey may be hard but stay the course. God's promises are on the other side of your surrender and obedience.

*Part 2*

———

# RELEASE

❧

# Chapter 5

## MY EXODUS

The following day, I woke up at four o'clock sweating profusely. I had a dream that I was in chains, and the only way I could be released was to dance for my life. The song Deliver me was still playing when I woke up. Instantly, the array of emotions that I felt earlier in the night returned as if they had never left. I remember asking God to free me and telling Him I wanted to live! I got out of my fetal position on the floor, where I fell asleep, and started dancing to the song. Little did I know that dance was one of my forms of praise, and I released a shackle with each sway.

Suddenly, I felt compelled to drive an hour and a half to my hometown to do this dance at the church I grew up in. As much as I did not understand the church, this was a great place where I felt safe and surrounded by people that genuinely cared for me. I had to choose to go out of obedience or ignore the clear assignment God gave me in a dream. I was telling God that I wanted to live and be free. This was God's way of honoring His word and determining how desperate I was for Him.

I was known for going to God when I wanted Him to do something for me and backing away once it was taken care of. It did not matter if God handled it or if I took matters into my own hands. If the situation was cleared, I no longer was concerned about how it was rectified or who was responsible. God knew that I could not afford to think that what I needed would be granted at once. This meant that I had to submit and surrender before God could show up in my life and honor what I asked of Him.

So, I decided to be obedient and call my pastor, requesting to dance at the ten o'clock Sunday service. Without hesitation, he agreed and was delighted to have me. I rode back to my hometown in silence, and the song, Deliver Me, incessantly played in my head. The enemy tried to plant seeds of doubt, and I started questioning everything about the trip. I had to work the next day, I did not have a dance choreographed, and this was the epitome of last minute. Despite my doubtful thoughts, I continued to drive.

When I got to the church, I fell into worship for the first time. Usually, I would look around the church and spectate before lifting my hands or singing. This time was different. When I stepped into the building, I had tunnel vision. I found a seat, threw my purse down on the pew, and started seeking out the presence that I had felt the night before. I came to church with an expectation, and I must say that it was met. I remember naturally lifting my hands and crying out when the phenomenal Wings of Faith choir sang Break Every Chain by Tasha Cobbs. This song resonated with me because I felt like I had invisible chains gripping hold of me. I could not see them, which is why I could not break myself free, but the song declared that an army was rising to break every chain. The leader of the army assigned to setting me free was Jesus. I felt at peace knowing I did not have to do this alone because an army was rising on my behalf.

The song ended, and I was an emotional wreck on the inside. Despite my inability to pull it together, it was my time to dance. I was so lost in emotion that I could not feel any nerves, and the only person that mattered at that moment was God. As I danced, I started to feel lighter. My second encounter with God was worthwhile and left me wanting more.

After church, I fellowshipped with the people who practically raised me. Adults came to me and talked about how they felt the Holy Spirit as I danced; all I could think was I did too. It was amazing to know that other people could identify with the feeling, and it confirmed that I truly did have an encounter with God. As I drove back home, the words of the song continued to play in my mind. I was ready to say goodbye to the old me, but I had to welcome a new version of myself. I had no clue who she was supposed to be. However, that was irrelevant because I came to know the God that created me.

Over the next few weeks, I started studying the Bible and watching sermons on YouTube, and I even found a church home where I lived. Finally, I was ready to do things differently and meet this new version of myself. Getting into the word of God was one of the hardest things I ever decided to do. My understanding was limited, and I felt like everything was foreign. So, I bought a devotional and a study Bible to help me go deeper into the Word. I naturally started reading the book of Exodus because it was heavy on my heart after repeatedly listening to the song by Le'Andrea. I knew that the Israelites were freed from Egypt, but I gained a new revelation after intentionally reading the Word of God for myself. It turns out I could relate to the Word more than I thought.

When reading about the Israelites and how they were treated in Egypt, I wondered why God would allow them to be treated that way. The Israelites cried out to God and were left to suffer, but I realized that was far from the truth. As I read about Moses, I learned that he faced death from the moment he was born. But on the other hand, I started to learn about the character of God. Despite what Moses experienced, God had His hand on him the entire time because Moses had a significant call on his life. One that he did not even know about until he encountered the burning bush. The Lord spoke to Moses plainly and acknowledged that He heard the Israelite's cries and called him to bring the Israelites out of Egypt.

Moses did exactly what many of us tend to do. He questioned God. He had a speech impediment and did not feel qualified to lead the Israelites out of Egypt. However, what we see as a deficiency does not stop God from using us. We must understand that our limitations do not limit our God. He will use anyone willing to do His will.

In Exodus 5:22, Moses asked why the Lord brought trouble to His people and why He had not rescued them as He promised. I started thinking about the times I felt alone and concluded that God had given up on me. The times when I began to doubt God's existence because I believed he left me during my times of trouble. As I continued to read, I realized that the Lord answered Moses and reassured him to stay the course. I started wondering if I ever truly listened to the Lord's response. I talked to God a lot, but I do not think I was ever quiet enough to listen. God had everything figured out, but to Moses and the Israelites, His plan appeared ineffective or nonexistent because God did not show up the way everyone expected.

Pharaoh did not want to let the Israelites go, and from his position, he thought he had the authority to make that decision. Knowing God's power, I expected Him to force Pharaoh to immediately free the Israelites, but that is not what happened. Everything about this exodus was intentional and a process that had to be carried out. God showed up in a way that I thought was cruel and unnecessary. He brought plagues of blood, frogs, gnats, flies, boils, hail, locusts, and darkness. He killed livestock and killed firstborns. I did not understand why God had to bring all this turmoil to free the people of Egypt. God revealed to me that sometimes what we experience is not meant for us to understand. We are just meant to recognize God's hand in the midst. God needed to prove to the Israelites that he heard their cries and show Pharaoh that God did indeed exist and was the supreme ruler of everything. The plagues were a way of humbling everyone and giving them a chance to acknowledge God once and for all.

God could have forced Pharaoh to bow to Him, which is what I expected Him to do. If that were the case, the Israelites would not have appreciated how God brought them out and could have taken credit for their release. I know that would have been my thought process. When I was at the lowest point in my life, I cried out to God and wanted Him to show up immediately. However, I did not realize how He answered my prayers all along. I did not recognize what God was doing because He did not operate on my timing and His tactics were the opposite of what I had in mind. God did not show up the way I expected Him to, and even after His presence was made clear, I still had work to do on my part. When Pharaoh finally let the Israelites go, they still had to decide to leave despite the obstacles that awaited them. Like their exodus, I had to leave fear behind and muster enough faith to follow God to freedom. This meant that I had to leave my old ways of thinking behind.

I could not take toxic relationships with me, depression had to stay behind, and I had to cross the sea of healing. I had no clue how I would get across, but I knew I had to go forward or turn back to the bondage that awaited me. Returning to the place I asked God to free me from seemed easier than pursuing this new way of life. Everything started changing, and I had to decide to choose God daily. I wanted the process quick and easy, but God does not operate that way. God is intentional, and His decisions are made in our best interest. When I wanted to go back to the man that brought me temporal comfort and satisfaction, I remembered that God was trying to heal me from the insecurities that made me seek superficial love in the first place.

The truth is that God knew my heart from the beginning and would not put more on me than I could bear. I always thought that scripture meant life would be easy, but that is not what God meant. As the Israelites were fleeing from Egypt, God sent them on a detour surrounded by desert, which was longer than the alternate route. Human perspective would lead me to question God again, but I realized He did that because He knew the minds of His people. God knew that the shorter route brought more problems and could cause the Israelites to turn back out of fear. Sometimes the shorter route is not the best way to go even though it appears easier from the outside looking in. At this moment, I realized that God knows me better than I know myself, and His plan is far greater than anything I could ever devise.

Everything that I faced in the past resulted from doing things my way. After meeting God and learning more about His character, I developed a faith in Him that brought peace that surpassed all of my human understanding. The next thing I had to cross was the sea of healing, which meant I needed to let go of everything that kept me bound. This process was not easy, and I am far from done. Keep reading to learn more about my journey to freedom and how I began accessing God's promises.

# Dear Reader

⁓

When you accept Jesus as your savior, you will have to leave anything behind that keeps you distant from Him. Like the Israelites, you have access to freedom. You have to decide to go after it.

God is your guide and will never leave you nor forsake you. Walking away from familiarity is hard but necessary. There is more that God has in store for you. If you want to see the promises of God unfold, you must forget the former things and stop dwelling on the past. God wants to do a new thing in your life.

Don't look back out of fear or regret. Look forward to a brighter tomorrow as you walk with your Heavenly father. Depression, anxiety, and fear may try to creep in, but allow that to draw you closer to God. Be honest with the Lord about your feelings and lay all your worries at his feet. Your exodus is a journey. No matter how the path looks, don't turn back! Keep your focus on Jesus, and you will make it to your destination of purpose, peace, healing, and freedom.

## Chapter 6

# VICES VERSUS VISION

⚮

For years I've been told that there is a calling in my life. My mom always said I would speak to the nations, and my Godmother, Ms. P, used every opportunity to remind me of this. As she put bows in my hair at age five, she told me that I was special and would be used by God. I had no clue what that meant, and it went entirely over my head. I knew of God, but I did not know Him for myself. They were able to see things that I was not aware of. Just like the devil could see what was on the inside of me. I believe he was intimidated because he tried his hardest to keep me from recognizing my true potential.

I remember watching Jekalyn Carr on stage singing, prophesying on YouTube, and telling my mom that I was supposed to do the same. Around the age of ten, this was the first time God showed me a glimpse of what I was called to do. So, I watched all her videos and was inspired by her spiritual walk. During that time, I started reading the Bible and leading my youth group at church. I recall going to a youth conference called "I Promise." They talked about remaining pure. I was excited to keep myself and wait until marriage to have sex. But, again, the devil saw how God was ordering my steps and started scheming, trying to get me off course. Well, he was successful.

When my dad left, I felt like a piece of my puzzle was missing, and anger enveloped me. Instead of following God's vision, I turned to vices. The devil used my parents' marriage to get to me, and it worked. My role model went from Jekalyn Carr to my best friend in middle school, who introduced me to pornography and masturbation. I went from one extreme to another - saving myself and speaking on stages for God to fantasizing in front of a computer screen about having sex. That is where my vices started, and I have been running from vision ever since. I did not keep my eyes fixed on God. Instead, I diverted toward the enemy's deceit.

My vices spiraled into addictions that I could not beat on my own. I lost my virginity at fifteen and found myself in relationship after relationship, looking for a sense of purpose and belonging. After being misused by men, my body became an object, and I had no sense of self-worth. At this point, I was introduced to drinking then marijuana, and I could not go a day without one. I no longer wanted to feel anything and enjoyed being numb to everything. There were moments when I could understand something clearly at last and wanted better for myself, but the slightest issue pushed me back into darkness. I saw glimpses of happiness that would never be sustained because the source was superficial. God was the only source that could supply everlasting joy, an eternal light that outshines any darkness we may experience.

Idolatry is a sin, and many of us fall into the enemy's trap because we choose to worship gods that only distance us from the one true God. When I look at the life of Jesus, He did not allow anything to get in between His relationship with the Father. We must be careful not to make idols out of God's creation because this removes our focus from the Creator. I have made more idols than I can count in less than a quarter of a century of life. I've worshiped men, jobs, clout, validation, sex, drugs, etc. None of it got me anywhere in life. These idols only subjected me to pain, heartache, disappointment, fatigue, and regret. However, something attracted me to the very things that God eventually delivered me from.

It turns out I was running from God's vision for my life. I knew what God wanted me to do: serve Him. However, serving God is hard when His vision for your life goes against the false vision we try to make for ourselves. So, I became a lukewarm Christian because I only served God when it was comfortable and convenient. I turned to vices when trying to turn my attention away from God. Sometimes I blatantly ignored God's direction because it was not conducive to my current plans. I was hardheaded, and if I am being honest, I still am. Writing this book is a prime example of me running from vision and turning to vices. Many days God would place it in my heart to write, and I would find time to do everything except for what God asked me to do. Let's just say God had something for that. He stopped giving me vision, which was the wake-up call that I needed. It's interesting how we can disregard vision when God allows us to see part of His plan and get worried when we can no longer see. God knew that if I could not trust Him with the vision, I would need to learn to trust Him without it.

God revealed to me that my trial period of our relationship had ended. I could no longer pick up and put God down as I pleased. During my trial period with God, He wanted to reveal His faithfulness, mercy, grace, provision, and unfailing love. I was still catering to my desires throughout the trials, following my own plans, and "living my best life." I was still living in sin and grateful because I knew God was keeping me. I even started going back to church to show my gratitude. This lasted for a few months until depression knocked at my door again. My trial with God was over, and it was time for me to access the subscription Jesus paid for. Meaning I could no longer settle for a touch from God. I had to decide to walk with Him. I was not ready for the storms, trials, and tests that came with following God. I resorted to my comfort zone many times, but God kept tugging at my heart, drawing me closer to Him.

Even when I turned away from God, I could not veer for long. After being in the presence of God and being born again, you no longer feel comfortable living a life of sin. God needed me to recognize that I was my greatest enemy, and deliverance would only be effective if healing came with it. I wanted God to fix my problems while God wanted to restore my soul. My fears superseded my faith, and I was only led by what I could see. I saw a broken woman trying to keep her head above water. My focus was on surviving while God was pushing me toward thriving. Often, we only focus on what is right in front of us, which prevents us from understanding the complexity of God's overall plan. Every vice we turn to only taints the vision God tries to reveal to us. Without vision, we will fail to see God's provision, and this will cause us to miss out on the intricate details of His divine plan.

When I think about the story of Moses, I realize that my spiritual vision was blurred because I was still at the bottom of the mountain I was meant to climb. Moses did not receive vision until he climbed Mt. Sanai and reached the top. The climb prepared him for the vision God was about to reveal. I avoided climbing my spiritual mountain because I did not want to leave familiarity, friends, and what I considered "fun." God wanted me to get closer to Him and tested my obedience. Having to distance yourself from close friends is difficult, especially when you still receive those invites to do what God is calling you away from. I tried stringing some people/things up my spiritual mountain, and I could never climb because they only weighed me down.

I remember asking God why the vision he showed me was unclear and not happening. God revealed my problem. I could not reach something that I was not close to. Getting uncomfortable was necessary to reach what God had for me. The closer I got to God, the clearer the vision would be. In my mind, I figured I could go after God and still live the same. I was not ready to let my vices go because they were my norm. Like many of us, I tried to take the easy way out. I expected God to bring the vision to me versus getting in reach of the vision. I did not want to replace my norm with uncertainty because of fear, doubt, worry, and lack of faith. I would start my spiritual hike by reading God's word and talking to God, but if God told me to do something I was uncomfortable with, I ignored him and returned to my comfort zone. If Moses chose to ignore God, he would have failed to lead the Israelites to the Promised Land. God could not trust me with the vision until I made an effort to get in reach of it.

The vision was attached to my obedience and my level of commitment to God. It is one thing to talk and listen to God. It is another to willingly submit to His will and act according to it. I knew what God was asking me to do. I just did not feel comfortable doing it. I was so afraid of the journey and assignments God was giving me that I avoided them. In my mind, the only way I could embark on the journey ahead was to bring my comfort with me because I feared being alone. I thought relationships with men would help me when they were genuinely hindering me. God revealed that I was trying to take the dead weight up my spiritual mountain. My relationship with God was not growing because my ex's presence drowned God's voice. I had more comfort in a relationship with a man than with Christ. That is the primary reason we must let go of any idol we put before God. Despite how hard it may be, know that you will never be able to climb your spiritual mountain until you release everything holding you back.

I honestly don't know how I expected God to give me more direction when I continued to neglect what he had already asked me to do. Instead, God showed me that my blessings and destiny were on the other side of my obedience. I would not have a clear vision or get closer to my purpose until I started doing what God said.

I knew that I could not afford to play with purpose, so I finally surrendered to God. I was saved and knew God, but He wanted me to see Him. Genesis mentions that we were made in the image of God. My vision was unclear because I could not see the image of God, meaning I never truly saw myself, and it never had anything to do with my sight. It had everything to do with God's will. How could I carry out the will of God when I didn't even know my true identity? Finally, as I began to see God, I saw myself and could turn away from vices and start ACTIVATING my vision.

# Dear Reader

⌘

The enemy sends vices to get you to veer away from vision. Don't fall into his trap. Temptation, greed, pride, betrayal, fear, and anger are some of the vices the devil tries to lure us into. They are blinders that block vision and prevent you from walking in purpose. Deception is overruled by truth. As you learn better, choose to do better. God loves you and desires to use you in His kingdom. Know that it is up to you to climb your spiritual mountain. An effort is required, and the climb may be uncomfortable, but the perspective and wisdom you will gain are worth it!

Your problems will appear small in comparison to the power of God. The enemy knows this, so he tries hard to weigh you down. Release those vices and allow God to replace them with vision as you seek Him. You are worthy, valuable, and loved by God. Don't ever allow anyone to convince you otherwise. If you are lost and don't know what to do next, turn to God. Start climbing that mountain by getting into the word of God, surrounding yourself with believers, and surrendering your heart to your Father. Soon, the scales will begin to fall from your eyes, and your vision will be clear.

# Chapter 7

## LET GO!

Saying goodbye to something or someone you have grown to love is one of the hardest things we must do as believers. I had difficulty understanding why God was calling me to let go of the things/people I found comfort in. After a long day, I relished the thought of being cuddled by a man and feeling comforted. The problem was that I confided in people more than God. It did not take long to discover that God is truly jealous. He knows that anything or anyone we look to more than Him becomes an idol. So many subconsciously make gods out of people, money, jobs, social media, titles, etc. The Bible clearly states a primary commandment that warns us not to put any other gods before our Heavenly Father.

My relationships did not work out, the money did not last, and the titles were not enough validation because it was all superficial. None of it meant anything, but it became the world to me. I found comfort in things that would only satisfy me for a short time. When walking with God, we must understand that He is our source of love, strength, guidance, peace, joy, sustainability, resources, and everything else we need. Without this perspective, we will make idols out of God's creation without crediting the Creator. When we place our faith in idols, they become our comfort zone.

God was calling me away from the comfort zone I idolized because it prevented me from becoming who God called me to be. I became complacent and comfortable with my job, my poverty mindset, my "friend boy" that I was entangled with, and the friends that I kept. I liked to party, get drunk, attract guys, and have a "good" time. However, that did not align with the assignment, gifting, or anointing over my life. So, the more I held onto that lifestyle, the further away I got from God and my overall purpose in life. Over time, I fell into depression again and began to worry about things without knowing why.

See, God can deliver us from one thing, and we will constantly stumble if we do not allow God to rip away every string that attached us to the stronghold in the first place. This process is painful, and we must have enough faith to push past the pain to get to the promise. Letting go was difficult, and I had to have enough faith to obey despite my feelings. Unfortunately, faith did not fall in my lap. I had to study the word of God, pray, worship, and get into an intimate relationship with God. During this process, God started revealing what was hindering me. Some of the music I listened to triggered lustful thoughts and contributed to my desperation for artificial affection. My "friend boy" was the connection to my insecurities, leading me to rehearse thoughts of not being good enough. I tried to find reasons why he did not want to be with me and attempted to change myself to meet his needs—failing to realize that there was nothing I could do to gain the love, attention, and affection of a man that was not meant for me.

Letting go was hard, but holding on was damaging my soul. I was attached to a man for three years because I had a soul tie with a knot, leading me to believe that one day everything would work out. I was sure he was supposed to be my husband, and I was willing to sin to make that happen. Shacking up, fornicating, and whatever else it took. I had no self-respect, morals, or security in my identity. My sin, insecurities, fears, desperation, etc., were like a magnet drawing me to him. God started ripping away everything that once attracted me to him. By the time God was finished, I could not go back if I wanted to because a relationship with him could only repel. As God ripped, I had to release, which is how God started healing me. After accepting Jesus Christ as my savior and receiving the gift of the Holy Spirit, God illuminated what was once dark. When you walk in the light, you will no longer feel comfortable walking in darkness.

Releasing is a significant part of healing, and we cannot do one without the other. They happen simultaneously. For example, when I let fear, rejection, disappointment, and unforgiveness out of my heart along with the strings that were disguised as people and things I found comfort in, God was able to start healing my heart. On the other hand, there are times when all I can do is cry out to God because the healing process is not pretty.

Early on in my spiritual journey, God started revealing that His word, prayer, praise, and worship were the tools that I needed to access healing. All of which I had minimal experience engaging in. I desired to heal but was unaware of the discipline I had to acquire to receive it. The mentality that healing should happen overnight will only lead to disappointment and repeated behavior. I had to be honest with myself and God to acknowledge the areas of my life that were keeping me bound. God exposed my brokenness, and I was in denial for a while, but I had to come to terms with the truth. To do that, I had to admit that I was living a lie. God also called me to let go of my false sense of perfection.

When crossing the red sea of healing, we must allow God into our hearts so the process can begin. Imagine stepping out into the ocean, not knowing how to swim, and having to trust that God will carry you through. That sounds crazy, I know. However, that is exactly what the Israelites had to do, and we must do the same. Stepping out into the water symbolizes having enough faith to allow God into our hearts. Many of us find this difficult because we have given our hearts to many people and were left broken, misused, abused, etc. So, we guard our hearts against everything and everyone, including God. During this season of my life, the mistake I made was treating God the same way I treated others that hurt me. My hardened heart was a defense mechanism and did not have an on-and-off switch. As a result, the pieces of my soul were shattered, and God was the only one that could make me whole. So, I prayed that God would come into my heart and restore me. Little did I know, the old version of myself would have to die for my God-given identity to be birthed.

It all started in March of two thousand twenty when everyone was locked into their homes due to a pandemic that shifted the construct of everyone's norm. I was looking forward to a cruise during spring break, but that was canceled along with the rest of my anticipated ventures. This was upsetting because I had many plans and did not know what to do in the house alone. But little did I know, that was exactly what I needed during that season of my life. I spent so much time catering to my family, students, coworkers, friends, and strangers - I rarely invested in myself. I remember walking around my neighborhood - the flowers were vibrant, the birds chirped melodies, and sun rays danced on my skin as I ambled in awe of God's masterpiece. Every day, I drove through this same neighborhood and never experienced it that way.

I would usually get home close to seven o'clock after leaving school. Exhaustion prevented me from noticing God's blessings right in front of me. A few days into lockdown, I started thinking about why I worked so hard. It was not about receiving accolades or recognition. It was my way of escaping my issues. Why would I stay at work for over twelve hours a day when I only got paid for eight? There were many opportunities to go home early, but I turned them down because I needed a time filler. Productivity was not the goal. I was just trying to keep myself busy.

Sadly, I would not have this perspective if I remained in the routine of life that I tranced into. I prayed for God to heal me but did not realize what I was asking for. If I did, I would not have prayed for it. After requesting healing in every one of my prayers, I started to think that God did not hear me. I stopped praying because I recognized that this monologue with Christ was not getting anywhere. After meeting God, I started going to Him about everything. Especially with the beef, I had with Him. I would begin asking God if He was listening to me. Why am I still in this position? God responded that the position was meant to prepare me for my purpose. My interpretation of healing was God removing all of my wounds. I just wanted to be happy, and I did not care what

God had to do for that to happen. I failed to realize that God was about to do some open-heart surgery, and there was no anesthesia except for His grace.

Over time I concluded that there is no such thing as freedom from pain or restraint. Have you seen this world? My anxiety could range from fearing death to staring death right in the face. Fear engulfed me, and the weapon that formed against me was close to prospering. Not because it came close but because my mindset was the grenade. Negative thoughts morphed into a stagnant mentality that felt impossible to shake. Until I recognized that God's will is not for me to perish but to have eternal life, this reminder helped me realize that my feelings were resurfacing because God was pointing me toward the root of my pain. Although, I must admit, revisiting my trauma was more painful than the original impact that caused the wound.

Neglect was the adrenaline that prevented me from feeling the initial pain in the first place. God showed me that I had to feel the pain to heal. Truthfully, it was frustrating, and I looked for ways to cope. I started looking for relationships again, but God began to convict me. He started revealing that any relationship I entered during that time would only contribute to my pain and delay my healing. Like many others, I ignored many of His warnings until another layer of rejection was piled on when the guy I turned to turned away from me. My disobedience reinforced what God said, and I finally understood that God wanted me to lean on Him versus the temporary comforts of this world.

After resorting to familiarity, I was reminded of why I had to let it go in the first place. The alternative was seeking God's face even more. So, I started reading the word of God more and reciting scripture in my prayers. It was my way of reinforcing and reminding God of His promises. I told God that I would trust in Him and lean not unto my own understanding while looking for Him to direct my path. I also stated that God would never leave or forsake me, even in trouble. The more I prayed, the stronger I felt. As the words exited my lips, my faith increased, and the Holy Spirit began to saturate my heart. At this point, I learned how to have a heart of worship. My worries decreased as my worship increased. There were countless times when I fell short and went back to my comfort zone, but trial and error can eventually lead to success if you keep trying.

# Dear Reader

⌘

**K**now that you are a part of a divine plan, and as long as you have breath in your body, you have another opportunity to experience God. Do not stop at the encounter or someone else's verdict on who God is. Define that for yourself through a personal relationship with Him. My journey to healing does not end with this book, but I am learning to accept the process.

Imagine realizing that your life is a product of everything you have experienced. What if you never experience God? Many encounter God but are not intentional enough to experience Him in His fullness. While asking God to heal me, I requested that He strip away every part of me that was not like Him. I resented that initially because everything I lost reflected what I spent my life trying to gain. But everything God blessed me with in return confirmed that I made the best decision.

Do not stray away from the promise because of your current position. Know that this is a season that will soon transition into another. When Fall comes, you cannot hold onto your leaves. Sometimes God has to get us bare to see what lies underneath. When God begins to remove things from your life (habits, people, accessibility, clout, etc.) He is revealing who you are without it. Embrace that and enjoy the journey to healing.

*Part 3*

———

# PROCESS

⧸⧹

# Chapter 8

## REJECTING RELIGION

ⷭ

When I turned away from God in the past, I was not upset with Him. I was fed up with religion. The problem was I could not tell the difference between the two. I thought religion was my access to God when that was not true. Anyone that can go to church for years and their heart remains in the same state of brokenness has not experienced God. They just mastered religion. As much as healing hurt, I was able to bear it because I entered into a love relationship with my Father. His love, grace, mercy, peace, and joy made up for my pain. I learned to tap into the Holy Spirit that lived inside me, where I found my strength.

My experiences in life set the stage for my experience with God. None of it made sense when I was going through it, but the pieces started to come together as I intentionally invested in my relationship with Jesus. Religion made me feel like I needed to be perfect before coming to God. My relationship with Jesus reminded me that God knew my weaknesses and wanted to love me through them.

God does not expect us to have it all together when we come to Him. He understands that we are flawed beings. That is why He sent

His son Jesus Christ to die on the cross for our sins. When I could internalize this, I stopped turning away from God and began leaning on Him even more. It is important that we realize where our help comes from because we cannot do this thing called life by ourselves. We die to ourselves, so we can be resurrected into the person God has called us to be. Our goal is to be more like Jesus, not merely a better version of our old selves. I always wondered how Jesus could be selfless, love those who persecuted Him and do everything God called Him to do. It was because he was in an intimate relationship with the Father. Jesus consecrated Himself, stayed in prayer, and consulted the Father in everything He did. We must do the same to carry out God's will.

After reflecting, I realized I left the church because it was like a revolving door. Nothing in my life was changing. No one was to blame for that, but I knew I had to do something different if I wanted a new outcome. Many Christians reach insanity because they repeat the same actions expecting different results. Religion focuses on the act while our relationship with God builds trust and understanding. We can pray, go to church, speak in tongues, and even tithe, but it means nothing if our heart is not in it, and we lack the wisdom to do what God intended. After meeting God, I longed to connect with Him in a way I never had. I intrinsically wanted to get to know God for myself and seek His face. Not because I was told but because I was desperate. On the other hand, I learned that desperation does not deepen our relationship with God. Desire does.

How do we transition from desperation to desire? I realized that my walk with God was inconsistent because I only sought after Him when I was desperate for something that I lacked. I was going back and forth with God because my relationship with Him was rocky initially. I had to do so much unlearning about who God is and how He operates. When we accept Jesus Christ as our Savior, that is not the finish line. That is where the relationship begins. The beautiful thing about God is His grace comes alongside our faith. We will mess up, fall off, and drift away - but our God remains the same. Our flesh is weak, but God's power is perfect in our weakness. If we want to veer away from desperation to desire, we must seek God with all our hearts and every part of our being.

The enemy tries to keep us distant from God, but the moment you decide to lay your anger, shame, frustration, and everything else concerning you at the feet of Jesus, all bets are off. Positioning our hearts toward God and releasing our worries should be our main priority because that will bring peace that surpasses all understanding. There is no need to try to make sense of our lives on our own because our connection to the Father is all the understanding we need. When you know that God created you with all power, there is no reason to fall victim to the mentality that the enemy tries to get you to trance into. Instead, *we begin to war according to the Holy Spirit that dwells on the inside of us and takes any thought into captivity that goes against the knowledge of God and make it obey Christ*, as it states in 2 Corinthians 10:5.

Coming to this conclusion was not ideal nor easy in the beginning, and I still struggle to this day. I learned early on that the plans I set for my life were not aligned with what God had for me. Talk about a hard pill to swallow. In hindsight, conforming to religion was more appealing to the flesh than having a relationship with God. When I conformed to religion, I learned how to follow the rules set for me. Was it ideal? No, but sin mixed with compliance was much easier than the consistency that comes with obedience.

However, the consequences were far worse and made me rethink every decision I ever made.

Living a life of sin felt good to my flesh but crushed my soul. I knew that I had to alter my way of thinking and actions if I wanted to live a life of purpose. Yet I did not know where to start. Growing up in the church leaves you with much knowledge, but wisdom and understanding only come through a relationship with God. Many people get frustrated with religion because you can learn what the Bible says without having the reasoning behind it. Making people feel like being a follower of Christ is delusional and far-fetched when that is not the case. I learned that following Jesus was a journey, not a formality. That is why God desires a relationship with us.

The God that everyone spoke of in church was not the God that I met. His Word remained the same, but our encounters were personal. How God showed up in someone else's life was not identical to how He showed up in mine. God knows what each of us needs and does whatever it takes to meet that need. I came to this conclusion after reading the Bible for myself. I learned about the character of God and how to lean on God in every area of my life. I started praying to God as if He were sitting next to me. Over time, God became my confidant, peace, comfort, shoulder to cry on, joy, love, and more. My relationship with God made letting go easy because I knew He was everything I needed.

Even with this new mentality, there were days when I started to feel distant from God when I allowed my flesh to come between us. However, that never lasted for long because nothing could separate me from the love of God. When I felt myself drifting, God pulled me back in with a reminder of His love. Every time I thought about where God delivered me from, I knew that I could not go back. It was through my relationship that I began to understand religion. It was never meant to turn into rituals that people did out of compliance. Instead, it was meant to reverence God and demonstrate our complete and total reliance on Him. With that knowledge, I stopped entering relationships aimlessly, stopped having premarital sex, and started seeing my value. None of this happened overnight, and I am evolving every day, but I am now on the right track, which matters most.

## Dear Reader

⌘

Religion can often blind you to who God is. No matter how hard you try, you will never be able to live up to every commandment on your own. God desires a relationship with you because He wants to take you on a spiritual journey where He will guide you to healing. As you heal, God will reveal his plans and promises. Then you will be able to see God for who He is. God is Yahweh, the great I Am. Meaning that He is everything that you could ever need. Your imperfection does not stop God from loving you and wanting to work in and through you.

I had to reject religion to meet and enter into a true relationship with God. Have you ever met Jesus? If you have complied with religious principles and your heart is still broken, it's time to seek a relationship. I challenge you to open your Bible, go into your prayer closet, and pour your heart out to God. You can pray, write, sing, dance, cry, or do anything else to express how you feel. As you pour, God will extract your pain, and once you have that initial encounter, you will never feel comfortable losing sight of Him again.

# Chapter 9

## THE TESTS

In school, I always loved tests at the recall level of understanding. I have always been good at memorizing information as I have a photographic memory. Every test that mimicked the study guide was my way of maintaining an A in my core classes. My test-taking method sufficed until I got to Chemistry class in the tenth grade. I panicked during my first exam because the test looked nothing like what we reviewed. Chemistry required me to apply what I learned in class, which is exactly how God tests me today.

Every time I pray for something - there is always a test to follow to ensure that I am ready to receive it. I asked for a husband, and let me just say, I am still working to pass the tests that come with that responsibility. For example, can I cook? Yes. Do I want to? No. I say that jokingly, but I know that is something God tests me with. I asked for a man who can chef it up in the kitchen, so I could avoid this task. This is a prime example of how I desire something while trying to push the responsibility that comes with the blessing onto someone else. I pray for a man that is loving, ambitious, God-fearing, genuine, compassionate, thoughtful, selfless, humble, and a great listener. I will not pretend like that is the end of my list, but Pastor Mike Todd told me to rip up the rest. So, this is my adjusted list of standards. With that being said, God convicted me so quickly. What will I bring to the table? If I'm being honest, I am a procrastinator with big dreams, anointed and fearful, and ambitious while lazy. How is God supposed to grant my prayer when I am in that state? I'm not saying my prayer is too hard for God, but the man God has for me would not be attracted to me in my state.

God tests us to see if we are truly ready for the blessings He promised us. Our lives were planned out before we entered our mother's womb. God is in control, and His will includes the intricate details of our lives. The problem is that we ask God for blessings while looking to the world for manifestation. After trying this method for years, I realized that I would never see success because I was failing or avoiding each test that God sent my way. When we are of the world, we have blinders covering our spiritual vision, which ultimately prevents us from walking by faith. In turn, we walk based on what we can physically see, which is a test. First, God wants to know if we trust Him, and then the test comes if He can trust us.

God will give us a test and examine our hearts as we take it. He is not interested in our ability to carry out what He asks of us. He focuses on our heart posture while we do it. The Bible says it is not by our might or power but by His Spirit. God knows the tree by the fruit that we bear. We cannot obey God without the fruit of the Spirit. I can think of all the times I failed God's test, and the temptation to follow the desires of the flesh is the primary reason. God tests us while the devil tempts us, but I thought God was responsible for both. I believed God was waiting for me to fail because why else would He allow the devil to tempt me? Then 1 Corinthians 10:13

made me realize that God would not let me be tempted beyond my ability, which was how He tested me. God tested me to see if I would turn towards Him or the enemy. Kingdom business is no joke, and God does not need fickle believers fighting on His behalf.

Every test comes when a lesson is taught; many of us forget what we learn when it's time to apply it. In my teenage years, I learned many lessons during my rebellion. Acting out was my way of communicating my frustration with God for not removing my suffering. After walking with Jesus, I know our suffering brings out our weaknesses, but it reveals God's strength. God's power is made perfect in our shortcomings. When God tested me in the past, I had a lot of knowledge but lacked wisdom, which is just the application of sound knowledge. Proverbs mention the Lord grants wisdom, but we must incline our ear to it. I failed many of God's tests because I still had to learn to trust and obey Him. I have come a long way, but I have not mastered this to perfection, and I never will. God just wanted me to focus on progression as I witnessed the transformation process I am still going through.

As I started learning what God desired, I felt like a failure every time I knew better but failed to do better. Shame and guilt dug a hole for fear to nestle in. Then I learned more about the character of God as I studied the Bible for myself. **Our Father is so loving that He cares more about restoration than retribution.** To the point where God extends His grace, and there is nothing we could ever do to earn it. The more God revealed himself to me, the more I desired to seek Him. The truth is, I never had a chance at passing any of God's tests on my own. Failure was my only option if I continued neglecting my inheritance as a child of God, which the enemy wanted me to do. Jesus walked this Earth with power, love, and boldness because He had keys to the Kingdom and was not afraid to use them. God sent Jesus as the perfect teacher because no test was too hard for Him. Jesus left a permanent imprint on every believer because He gave us access to God through the Holy Spirit.

Every test that God placed in front of me was just an opportunity for me to exercise my faith. God wanted me to tap into His strength, comfort, love, joy, peace, and anything else I needed. His expectation was never perfection, just an intimate love relationship with me so He could use me as His vessel. Getting to this point is a test in itself. When God told me to let go of my past, he was not forcing me to abandon the people I once loved. He just needed me to make room for where He was taking me, and as I looked back on my life, the tests reminded me of Abraham offering up his son Isaac. Was it ideal? No. However, he trusted God enough to let go of what he loved even when he did not understand. That is the epitome of faith, and that was all God needed. Abrahams's faith was confirmed at that moment. **Sometimes tests are just God's way of confirming your faith to ensure you are ready for where He leads you next.**

# Dear Reader

⧽

If you find yourself constantly failing the tests of God, check the foundation of your faith. Sometimes we get caught up in our everyday lives and go into survival mode when faced with a challenge that goes against our comfort. This mindset is rooted in fear and can only breed failure. Before passing a test, we must learn and study. Be a student, absorb knowledge, and incline your ear to wisdom. This translates to gaining more intimacy with God and tapping into His presence, power, and plans. We can't pass God's test without consulting and obeying Him.

We must understand that faith and fear cannot coincide because one will override the other. Whenever we are hesitant about what God calls us to do or question our abilities, we tell God that we do not trust Him. God knew you would not pass every test, so His grace covers the times you fall short. However, this is not an excuse to keep failing. Especially when you are equipped to pass, all you must do is tap in. When faced with a challenge, talk to God, and He will show you what to do. All we must do is follow while leaving the flesh behind. That is the actual test.

# Chapter 10

# OBEY OR DELAY

❦

One of the most challenging lessons I have learned throughout my life is obeying God. Truthfully, it is not easy to obey commands that go against the plans that you have set for yourself. Imagine working toward a specific goal your entire life and being directed away from it when you feel you are getting close. Anyone that has blood pumping through their veins would wonder why God would lead them in a direction that appears to be opposite of where they were headed. If you are anything like me, I questioned God, asking Him why He would allow me to get so far just to have me walk away. Unfortunately, I often ignored God and continued paving my own path, failing to realize that the longer I disobeyed God, the more I delayed my destiny.

Obedience requires submission, and I was not good at agreeing to things I did not understand. I spent most of my life doubting myself, procrastinating, and turning down opportunities. My default answer to anything God called me to do was "no" until I felt comfortable saying yes. The problem was that I rarely felt comfortable submitting to God's plans because I only acted on what I could see. I avoided any task that seemed impossible or felt out of reach. The Bible says that we must walk by faith and not by sight. I was doing the exact opposite and was led down the path of destruction because the enemy's deceit blinded me. My insecurities, fears, and failures were the only things I could see. So, I based all my decisions on that and disregarded what God called me to do.

During my third year of teaching, God called me back to school for my master's degree in Educational Leadership. Getting another degree sounded good in theory, but all I could see was an increase in student loans and another certification test I would have to pass. After failing my teacher certification test four times and finally passing on the fifth try, I convinced myself that I was perfectly content with being a teacher for the rest of my life. However, God had other plans because He kept confirming that I needed to return to school. So, I applied to the University of Tampa (UT), and within three weeks, I received an acceptance letter. I found it ironic because I was rejected from the University of South Florida when I desperately wanted to go after high school, but I was instantly accepted to the University of Tampa when I was reluctant. I remember feeling underwhelmed while staring at the packet in the mail congratulating me on the journey that awaited. After telling my parents the news, I stuck the letter in a basket sitting on the top shelf of my bedroom closet and left it there for three months.

On June 29, 2020, I realized that I had less than 5 hours to make a decision. I received an email from UT informing me that it was the last day to register for classes. After scrolling past the dozen other reminders weeks prior, I knew I could not afford to look past this final call to action. The school year was about to start, I was preparing to teach during the pandemic, and God was calling me to return to school. As much as I did not want to return, I had two options. Obey or delay. I had no clue what I would be delaying if I did not register, but I did not want to take the risk. So, I registered for classes, and a week later, I received my first syllabus for grad school. I recall telling God that He would have to carry me through because there was no way I could make it on my own. Little did I know, that was exactly what He wanted to hear.

The beautiful thing about obedience is that when God directs us to do something, He wants to do the work through us. When I think about the times I failed in the past, it was because I tried to do things on my own. God was teaching me to rely on Him, seek His face, and surrender to His will despite my feelings. Many nights tears poured onto my keyboard as I attempted to meet the criteria on the seemingly never-ending rubrics. As much as I wanted to quit, I knew I couldn't. So, I kept pressing as my pastor always encouraged us to do. Focus, fight, and finish were the three words that permeated my mind whenever I considered throwing in the towel. I may have left the church, but what I learned in the church did not leave me. I guess that is the result of being trained up as a child. With every A, I gave God the glory and found the courage to continue. Before I knew it, I had finished my last class, completed my internship, and applied for graduation.

Just when I thought I passed the test of obedience, God sprung another directive my way. God called me to leave the teaching field without telling me what was next. I started packing my classroom, and He led me to give everything away, which did not make sense because I did not see myself leaving teaching forever. So, again, I had to choose to obey or delay. After listening to God, an opportunity in Atlanta opened up, and I was excited because I felt like everything was starting to make sense. I applied, interviewed, and received a job offer within three days. The company wanted me to move to Atlanta and start training two weeks later. So, I went to God and asked Him to confirm if that is where He wanted me to go while I started making plans for the move. In my mind, I already told God "yes" without Him ever asking for it. Let's just say this opportunity was a good idea, but it was not a God idea, as Tiffany Buckner would say.

**I have learned that just because it looks good doesn't mean it's good for you.** In my mind, I had an apartment awaiting me, a job that paid more, and an opportunity to explore a new city. This was a prime example of me walking based on what I saw. A year before this, God called me to leave the classroom and move back home with my parents. Moving back home made me cringe, and I disregarded the idea whenever it tried to enter my mind. What would a 23-year-old look like moving back home? I was more concerned with the opinions of others than the plan of God. Ideally, I wanted people to think that I had life figured out. In reality, I had no clue what I was doing and was miserable trying to put the pieces together. Being a teacher was a dream come true, but after three years, I knew that there was something else that I needed to do. I just did not know what that was. So, God pushed me to leave the classroom and did not provide any details regarding what was next.

Before I leave one opportunity, I always want to have another one lined up. Atlanta was the next opportunity, and I was excited to go. Yet, that is not what God wanted, and He made that clear by staying silent when I was seeking confirmation about the move. So, I turned down the job and officially quit teaching without knowing what was next. At this point, I was embodying the meaning of walking by faith. I moved back to Miami with my parents, and I remember crying in my room because I felt like a failure. I spent my teen years trying to rush life just for God to slow me down and put me right back where I ran from. Home. Although this decision was not ideal, it was necessary.

After a few weeks, I thought God would send me a new job offer. So, I applied to several jobs on Indeed and waited for one of the employers to call me back. Instead, I received continuous rejection emails indicating that I was no longer being considered for the position. I knew I was qualified for every job I applied for, but I was denied every time. God was trying to teach me another important lesson. A temporary "no" is better than a premature "yes." During this specific season of my life, God needed me to focus on Him and nothing else. I had too many distractions that I idolized, so God stripped me of everything so I would remember that He was all I needed. In theory, this sounds good but losing everything your flesh desires is annoying.

This season was critical because God was trying to get my foundation right. I built my life based on the expectations of others versus God's will. Everything changed when I moved back home because my pride went out of the window. I finally surrendered my life to God and submitted to His plans versus my own. God wanted me to serve Him, and that is what I did. I stopped aimlessly reading the Bible and started studying His word while allowing the Holy Spirit to speak to me. I started being convicted, and God revealed areas of my life where I needed deliverance and healing. I needed deliverance from the imposter syndrome that my life was centered around. I felt like I was not good enough while trying to prove that I was externally. God was trying to show me that pleasing people would never satisfy me because I was not created to appease others. I was created to glorify God and allow Him to carry out His will through me. So, I chose to obey because I refused to delay what God had for me. I sat at the feet of Jesus for three months learning how to regulate my emotions, release my pain, and rely on Him. I felt like Hannah, weeping my way into worship. I learned how to be vulnerable before God, pray without ceasing, cast my cares, and praise and trust Him in the midst of my storm. This is where God wanted me to be, basking in His presence.

During this time, I started posting what God was teaching me on social media, not realizing that it was God's way of transitioning me into ministry. I was not seeking out followers or anyone else's approval. Before this, my feed was full of thirst traps, and I was using my body to seek the approval of men. It was my way of convincing myself that I was beautiful and worthy. However, my intentions for posting were different this time, and so was the outcome. I started telling people about God and how he transformed my life. As I released my story publicly, God reached the hearts of many others. Everything God was doing in my life was foreign to me but divinely orchestrated. The route God took me on was not ideal, but it prepared me for His promises (just like the Israelites).

After a few months, I applied for a job teaching one day per week after-school. I just needed something to do because I missed teaching, and I shared that with God. When I went on the interview, I thought it was for the after-school position, but God had other plans. The woman that interviewed me asked if I was interested in being a Director for the company. I never saw that coming. I sat in silence after the Zoom call because I knew that it was nobody but God. At that moment, I understood why I needed to return to school, leave teaching, and move back home.

My dad calls me the marriage counselor, which is ironic because I know nothing about relationships. However, God used my mom and dad to teach me what He can do in a marriage if He is at the center. Witnessing my parents learn how to love one another is a blessing because I stopped thinking it was possible. God brought me back home so I could stop harboring and heal.

Obedience is critical in our walk with Jesus. We must be hearers and doers of God's word. I will admit that we will not always have the complete blueprint of God's plan, but He will give us what we need along the way. For example, I did not understand why I needed to move back home, but now I do. God wanted to restore my family, put me back in the church that I grew up in, and give me a better job that I was never qualified for on my own. What I once blamed God for, I now thank Him for restoring, and it all came down to my obedience.

# Dear Reader

Obedience is better than sacrifice because it requires pure intent and faith. God has plans to prosper and give you hope and a future. We can access those plans by obeying the voice of God. Know that God will not lead you astray, and trust that He has your best interest at heart. Whatever God is leading you to do may not make sense now but stay the course. A wise woman once told me that the road may be wide now, but as you follow the voice of God, it will become narrow.

Many are called, but few are chosen. God has chosen you for a specific purpose. Will you choose to obey Him or delay what He has for you? The choice is yours. This journey with Jesus has challenges, but it's worth it! If you focus on fearing the Lord, which is reverently obeying Him, you will eventually see the promises of God unfold before you. *Eyes have not seen, nor ears have heard the things God has prepared for those who love Him* (1 Corinthians 2:9). This translates to, "you ain't seen nothing yet," as my momma would say. Draw closer to God and allow Him to order your steps while choosing to take them.

*Part 4*

---

# MOVE FORWARD

# *Chapter 11*

## FREEDOM

❦

What does the word freedom mean? When you have never experienced it, I know it is hard to define. A song says, "no more shackles, no more chains, no more bondage, I am free… yeah!" I sang it countless Sundays and was not able to relate. I always wondered how others around me got free from their issues, but they rarely shared that. The time for testimonies in church was always cut short while the sermon was extended. Testimonies helped me more than the sermon because it was the real-life application of the word, and I could hear the outcome versus suspect what would come next on my own.

The key to freedom is being honest about our issues, releasing them to God, denying the flesh, and taking on the mind of Christ. For years I held onto my pain as if not acknowledging it would make it all go away. Instead, the effects of my trauma intensified, and my soul was in a grave while my physical body went through the motions of life. After meeting God and entering into a love relationship with Him, I learned the true meaning of freedom - surrendering my entire being to Christ and allowing Him to transform me without allowing the enemy's deceit to prevent me from carrying out my purpose. There is so much fulfillment in doing what God has called you to do. I was in bondage because I did not believe I possessed the strength or strategy to execute the dreams and visions that God showed me. So, I ran from my calling and purpose versus pursuing it.

I have learned that freedom does not mean we are free from suffering. Trials and tribulations are inevitable and essential parts of our Christian walk. Our flesh despises suffering, while our spirit embraces it because our pain forces us to lean on God even more - which is where our help comes from. Understanding that you are connected to the Father, and He will never leave you nor forsake you is all the freedom we need. Life will bring worries and troubles, but our eternal peace comes from our Heavenly Father, and we are reminded of this truth when we think of Jesus. There is so much beyond this life, but God wants us to live it more abundantly while we are still here. We cannot afford to allow the devil or people to strip us of what God has placed in us.

The enemy comes to kill, steal, and destroy. If we know this, why do we choose to participate in his agenda? I could not access freedom because bondage was normal. I was consumed with familiar spirits and failed to see how they contributed to my demise. Generational curses made freedom feel unattainable, which was the enemy's plan. However, I was a willing participant in many of his schemes. For most of my life, I did not recognize how the devil was training me to do his job for him. The enemy wanted to steal my voice, kill my dreams, and destroy my character. His tactics were subtle and flattering to my flesh. I started comparing myself to others, which made me feel behind in life, causing me to shut down or overcompensate for what I felt I lacked. I also focused my attention on the opinions of others which led to seeking validation before everything I did.

Any seed that the devil plants can only grow if the soil is conducive for the seed. The soil represents our hearts which is connected to our minds. My mind kept me from being free. The moment I let my guard down and allowed God to come into my heart, my life changed. God blessed me with a new outlook on life and started uprooting everything the devil planted in me. Uprooting my comfort zone brought pain like none other, and the truth is that this process never ends. God will have to uproot anything that takes up the space He wants to dwell. I did not want to let the relationships go, the vices brought me comfort, and fear was familiar. However, those were just hindrances. When God started stripping those things, I felt like I was losing myself. In hindsight, I lost the counterfeit version of myself as God exposed my true identity.

After growing up in a household where everyone internalized their pain, I learned to do the same. I did not know how to be vulnerable and speak up for myself, so I remained quiet. Now I know this was the devil's way of stealing my voice. Muting me was his scheme, and he knew I could not reverse the damage he did on my own. For many years, I suffered in silence. I tried using relationships as an outlet, even though that only contributed to the enemy's overall plan. The devil stole another part of my being every time I laid with a man. When I turned away from God, I permitted the devil to take what God planted inside me. His plan worked until God revealed my purpose. As I let go of familiarity, God took my voice back from the enemy and unmuted me. Telling my story allows me to expose the enemy, share my testimony, and reminds me to keep going even when I am tempted to turn back. I found liberty in releasing my pain which was always part of my purpose.

Letting go of pain made room for the dreams that the devil tried to kill. Dreams that were dead started coming back to life, and I felt as if I could accomplish them. Fear prolonged my purpose because I was too scared to try. I always wondered why it was so hard to write this book. The devil planted fear because he knew it would kill my dreams. Throughout my relationship with God, he revealed the meaning of faith. Hebrews 11:1 (KJV) states, *"Faith is the substance of things hoped for, the evidence of things not seen."* I thought I needed all the details before pursuing my dreams, but faith taught me that hope was all I needed. I had to try even though I would not always see the evidence of my efforts. So, I started typing my heart out for over two years, and when I wanted to give up, I was reminded that the evidence might not be seen, but my efforts were not in vain. It took a while to write this book because my journey to healing, deliverance, and freedom did not happen overnight. I am still in the process and will remain in it until Jesus returns. Until then, I will continue to live out my dreams and do what God has called me to do.

Lastly, the devil tried to destroy my character, which made me feel distant from God. I knew I could not hide anything from God, so shame caused me to run from Him. I justified my actions by blaming God when I knew He was not at fault deep down. Sin put me down a rabbit hole, and I felt like there was no end. I became depressed, angry, bitter, envious, prideful, judgmental, etc. I believed God did not want anything to do with me in that state. Religion made me feel like I was sinful and broken beyond repair. I tried fitting the mold by doing everything right, but that did not last.

So, I started pretending to be perfect, and everyone celebrated my superficial nature while I was dying on the inside. Finally, I met God at my lowest point, realizing that He desired my heart even though it was out of order. God wanted my heart in its current condition and longed for a relationship with me. When I surrendered my life to Christ and became a true disciple, I was finally free.

# Dear Reader

꧁

Suffering, pain, disappointment, rejection, abandonment, fear, etc., were never meant to destroy you. The devil wants to make you think that you are not strong enough to overcome obstacles, but that is your nature. I know trials are not ideal when going through them, but you will come out stronger than you did when you went in. Remember, there is peace in your release, so do not bottle up your pain. Instead, seek therapy, consult a spiritual leader God leads you to, pray, and cry! Men, this is for you too. Cry! Let it out because holding it in will only quench the thirst of demons.

God is not looking for perfection. He wants you to enter into His presence and surrender everything to Him. Our flesh does not produce fruit. The Holy Spirit does. So, lean on God and not on your own understanding. The devil disorients our sight, so we will do his job for him. Pray for discernment, ask God to lead you, and order your steps. You will no longer be a slave to the enemy's schemes. I pray that your dreams be resurrected, your voice become unmuted, and your character be restored in Jesus' name.

# Chapter 12

## ACTIVATED!

The time is now! This was the word God continuously put on my spirit because I procrastinated in every area of my life. After being freed from depression, anxiety, and fear, nothing else could stop me from doing what God called me to do. So, I felt deep conviction about executing the things God placed on my heart. I dreamed that I was on a boat sitting by the water, finishing my first book. So, the following day, I randomly booked a cruise to the Bahamas a few days before I was supposed to walk across the stage to receive my master's degree. After reluctantly returning to school and finishing with a 3.8 GPA, I should have run across that stage. Yet, I did not have the desire to be recognized in that capacity. I wanted to celebrate on my own terms and accomplish another dream of mine.

I knew that graduating was proof that I could overcome my fears if I had the faith to face them. So, I decided to turn another one of my dreams into reality and complete the book I had worked on for over a year. For the longest, I beat myself up for not adhering to my set deadlines. Failing to realize that everything happens at the right time and God's promises do not have to be rushed. I could not write the book during my timeline because God was still writing my life story, and it would be incomplete if it were released prematurely. Now, I understand that God gave me the title of this book in a dream which symbolized the birth of my true identity. Deliverance, healing, overcoming vices, letting go of my past, rejecting religion, and choosing obedience were all necessary to get to this point in my life.

The journey has not been easy, but worth it. I attended a conference in Orlando that activated me. Before the conference, I felt so much pressure trying to do what God called me to do. I started speaking, writing this book, posting on social media, and walking into ministry. After a few months, I started feeling a lot of pressure trying to keep up with this new lifestyle. To the point where I tried to bring God along with me as I attempted to walk in obedience. The name of the conference was "Unleash," and I completely understand why that name was selected. After each worship service and workshop, I attended, God gradually unleashed me from the pressures I was carrying. Every boulder of perfection, inadequacy, opinions of others, and lack of knowledge were broken off of me. Some may ask how? During the last worship session that I attended, everything God imparted through His vessels hit me at once. Nothing matters except my relationship with God because everything else is impossible without it. God called me back to His feet and reminded me that He is my center. I was trying to walk in purpose by my false sense of power, which brought pressure. It's not by might nor power, but by His spirit! I started living my life believing I could do all things with Christ, but that is not what the Bible says. We can do all things through Christ! To be ACTIVATED, we must have a genuine connection with Jesus, the only way to the Father.

I thought this book would be about meeting God and my initial encounter with Him. The truth is that life is less about meeting God and more about knowing Him. Many people leave the church or

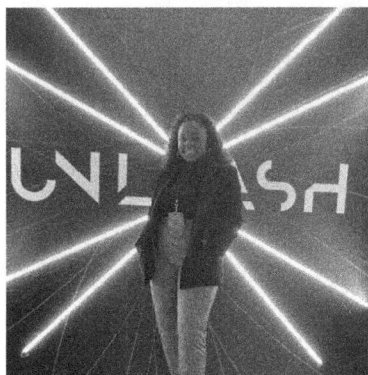

walk away from God because they never go beyond their initial encounter with Him. Causing them to think that God only shows up occasionally because they cannot identify His presence. God never leaves us, but we will not see how He is moving in our lives when we reject Him. My friend Mie kept repeating her motto for 2022, "Don't miss it!". A powerful word that we all need don't miss God!

My muzzle is gone, and my fear is fading. The devil had me quiet, but God is unmuting me. The old version of myself is in the grave where Jesus rose from. The grace of God has resurrected me. It is time to walk boldly and come for everything God promised me! The imposter syndrome, the spirit of comparison, and victim mentality must flee. I am ACTIVATING everything that God created me to be! God, it's nice to finally meet— know you!

# Dear Reader

—————

M y story does not end here, and neither does yours. God has a significant plan for your life, one that you will never be able to fully comprehend. However, His spirit will lead and guide you along the way. God wants your surrender and targets the heart. Even if your heart is broken, God still loves you. He is the mender of the brokenhearted and has the power to restore and resurrect you back to life. Don't allow the devil to deceive you and keep you distant from your heavenly Father. I don't know where I would be without Jesus, and I will spend the rest of my life sharing the Good News! We are not bound by death or slaves to sin as children of God.

God is not worried about what you've done wrong. He is not focused on your sin but on your salvation. He wants you to turn to Him and surrender all. Jesus had you in mind on the cross. He died for you! Accept Jesus and watch Him transform you from the inside out. There will be suffering in this walk, but with God, you are equipped to handle it. The challenges you encounter will increase your strength. God is so faithful and holds all power! Need more evidence? I challenge you to seek Him for yourself.

www.ingramcontent.com/pod-product-compliance
Lightning Source LLC
Chambersburg PA
CBHW072203090426
42740CB00012B/2367